BEGINNING MARKETING FOR THE PROFESSIONAL PUBLISHER

Business for Breakfast, Volume 11

BLAZE WARD

Knotted Road Press

Beginning Marketing for the Professional Publisher
Business for Breakfast, Volume 11
Copyright © 2019 Blaze Ward
All rights reserved
Published by Knotted Road Press
www.KnottedRoadPress.com

ISBN: 978-1-64470-048-8

Cover and interior design copyright © 2019 Knotted Road Press
http://www.KnottedRoadPress.com

All rights reserved. Except for brief quotations in critical articles or reviews, the purchaser or reader may not modify, copy, distribute, transmit, display perform, reproduce, publish, license, create derivative works from, transfer or sell any information contained in this book without the express written permission of Blaze Ward or Knotted Road Press. Requests to use or quote this material for any purpose should be addressed to Knotted Road Press.

Disclaimer
This book is provided for general educational purposes. While the author has used her best efforts in preparing this book, Knotted Road Press makes no representation with respect to the accuracy or completeness of the contents, or about the suitability of the information contained herein for any purpose. All content is provided "as is" without warranty of any kind.

Never miss a release!
If you'd like to be notified of new releases, sign up for my newsletter.

I will never spam you, or use your email for nefarious purposes. You can also unsubscribe at any time.

http://www.blazeward.com/newsletter/

Also by Blaze Ward

The Jessica Keller Chronicles
Auberon

Queen of the Pirates

Last of the Immortals

Goddess of War

Flight of the Blackbird

The Red Admiral

St. Legier

CS-405
Queen Anne's Revenge

Packmule

Persephone

Additional Alexandria Station Stories
The Story Road

Siren

Two Bottles of Wine with a War God

The Science Officer Series
The Science Officer

The Mind Field

The Gilded Cage

The Pleasure Dome

The Doomsday Vault

The Last Flagship

The Hammerfield Gambit

The Hammerfield Payoff

Doyle Iwakuma Stories

The Librarian

Demigod

Greater Than The Gods Intended

Other Science Fiction Stories

Myrmidons

Moonshot

Menelaus

Earthquake Gun

Moscow Gold

Fairchild

White Crane

***The Collective* Universe**

The Shipwrecked Mermaid

Imposters

Author's Note

First things first, I need you to take off your Author hat and put on your Publisher hat.

Yes, that means you.

What follows is not for the author. If you can't separate you: the author, from you: the publisher, you have bigger problems than I can help you with. I will occasionally address things that are author-specific, but the plan is to always return to how to market your writing as a publisher, rather than what you should write.

Second thing, I HIGHLY recommend you read the Business For Breakfast book: *The Beginning Professional Publisher*. I'm not going back over that document, so anything that appears in both places is purely accidental on my part.

Third thing, this book is more or less entirely dedicated to Indie Writers engaging in the Independent Author/Publisher Revolution. There are folks out there who are dedicated to following a Traditional Publishing Career Path. Almost nothing in this book will help you, because those folks are still trapped in a business model that dates to the 1970s or maybe 1980s and is dying under the weight of bad decisions made then, an inability to understand that they need to do to adapt now, and their

Author's Note

impending doom at the hands of corporate bean counters who demand a higher return on investment than publishing traditionally can get (14% when 7% is historically reasonable). In short, they are eating the seed corn today (2019) and if you don't reconcile yourself to that, you might never have any career as a writer.

I'm not going to sugarcoat things here, because most of you would prefer a straight answer that helps you with your career over someone blowing sunshine up your *****. I also swear occasionally, and I'm not sure how much of that language my editor will retain, so the previous line might be starred out by the time you read this.

Understand this: The world has changed.

Today (January 2019), we are in the middle of what my friends and I have loosely calculated as the seventh phase of the Indie Revolution, going back to about 2007 when Amazon launched the kindle as a full thing.

Each phase generally rotates around some new technology that makes things easier, either for the author, the publisher, or the reader; from the first kindles that allowed us to put up books without having to go through Traditional (New York City) Publisher. There is no agreement on the individual breakdowns, so I won't try to list them, but the release of the Vellum software and the rise of Do-It-Yourself Bundling on BundleRabbit (www.bundlerabbit.com) changed things tremendously by putting power in my hands, and that's the current phase. I'll talk more about them later on, and by the time you read this, we will have probably moved on.

Some of what I say here will be outdated soon. Probably not as much as the next volume I plan to write (Marketing for the *Intermediate* Publisher), because this book is intended to nail down the basics and those really don't change much or quickly.

Author's Note

I can't guarantee that by following all of the things I checklist below you will get rich and famous, but I'm pretty sure I can guarantee your failure if you don't. That's because these are the basics that separate the café dilettante in their berets from the professionals. If you aren't trying to understand at least this much, then you aren't serious.

In a brighter vein, many of these things should be things you nod at as you read, because someone else, somewhere, came along and gave you good advice on how to handle your Indie career and you listened. Go you.

So, Author hat off. Publisher hat on.

Or, as we liked to say back in the bad, old days: get in, sit down, shut up, and hang on.

Some Basics

You: The Author, The Brand

You have written a book. Or maybe lots of them. If your next step in the career success plan involves querying an agent, put this book back on the shelf and keep shopping. I can't help you. Sorry. However, if you want to go Indie, you're in the right place.

In the old days, the author was not the brand (not unless they were a *Big Name Author*). The publisher was the brand, because the publisher had a team of sales reps that made sure your book got into the bookstores around the country, tailoring their lists to the regional needs of their clients, who were the bookstores, not the readers.

Those days are largely done. TradPub (you will also hear me refer to "New York" in a derisive shorthand that means the same thing, namely the [as of today] Big Five Publishers traditionally headquartered in New York City or thereabouts) is no longer working at the local level. Bookstore chains are all about the latest bestseller, and not the so-called midlist that used to be where most professional authors could make a nice, middle class living.

Gone. Poof.

Let's touch on that again. Traditional Publishers were a Business-to-Business (B2B) industry, selling to bookstores and chains. One of their current failures is an inability (or unwillingness) to transform into a Business-to-Customer model (B2C) where they sell their books to the reader directly. This is why I don't seem them ever recovering from the tailspin they are currently in.

In their place, we (you and I) have eliminated the gatekeepers, and the middle man. You are now proposing to be your own Publishing company and get your books in front of readers with money burning a hole in their pocket. "**B2C**"

As a result, you need to understand that you are the brand. You. Jane Blow Author. Readers will follow *you*. They will buy *your* books. They will give you reviews for other readers. (Some of said reviews will even make sense and make you happy, but let's just step delicately past that for now.)

You are the brand. What you write is a style, a sensibility, a thing that brings in the readers. In the old days, a single TradPub writer might be forced to have a number of pennames under which she wrote. (My sister-in-law has five that I'm aware of, and a number of others *nobody* knows.) She wrote fast, then as well as now, as well as crossed genres, both major marketing problems for New York in those days. (And today, but that's a different book.)

The need for pennames today is greatly reduced in Indie, and often (IMO) counter-productive.

SIDELINE: Occasionally, I will insert thoughts like this because I'm writing this as a stream of ideas and notes, rather than a detailed outline I have spent a lot of time cleaning up.

FIRST RULE OF INDIE PRESS: *You are responsible for your own career*. Things that work for me might not work for you. They might not make any sense. If you don't like them, consider the implications they bring, and if you still don't think they help your career, ignore them. Ignore anything I say in this book if you need to, but understand *what* I said and *why*, so you have a good idea what you should do instead. Okay?

Getting back to pennames. You are the brand, so if you create a new penname for every book or every series that you write, you will have to build your fanbase from scratch every single time. There are reasons you might use pennames. Amazon will sometimes give you advantages in their algorithm as a result of being a "brand new author" but I find it to be a pain in the ass to keep track of.

CAVEAT: If you write erotica, I highly recommend that you have an erotica penname separate from your genre fiction penname. It will save you grief later.

You are the brand. Treat your name like a thing that must be jealously guarded. On social media, I walked away from just about all political ranting because I didn't want to potentially alienate half or more of my fan base. Now I just share things that make most people giggle out loud. I am a brand and I have to act like it.

If you're writing something with a very political bent, go for it. Just keep it in your fiction. Remember, on social media, fans lost don't ever come back. Understand those costs **before** you have to pay them accidentally. Or have two, unrelated social media names and deal with it that way. I don't, for reasons I'll explain in the next section.

WIBBOW

This is an acronym given to me by someone I respect and like and it has served me well. It stands for:

Would I Be Better Off Writing?

Everything I'm going to talk about here in the realm of marketing takes up your time. Everything you attempt (win or lose) takes away from your writing efforts. I don't know your pain threshold for marketing, but I suspect that it will be low at the beginning. That's okay. Much of what is in this book either won't take much time to do, or can be largely done once and then left on autopilot.

Find your happy level of marketing and stick with it for a while. Eventually, you can do more, but if you only look over this book and make a prioritized list for when you'll get to something, that's already a win for your career. Treat it as such.

The worst thing you can do is overwhelm yourself with all of this and freak out. Most of you are mid-functioning introverts at best, so disturbing your established patterns is *a bad thing*. I understand. There exist folks with the new job title "Virtual Assistant" that you can hire to handle some of this. WIBBOW sometimes translates into spending money to have someone else do it for you. Find someone reputable and ask for client references first, though. Some of those people won't work for you, and some of them are just con artists. The one my wife, Fabulous Publisher Babe™, uses works well with and for her.

Fear

The next topic we need to touch on is here because many of you have a very wrong-headed approach to being a professional writer and it will cost you later. You suffer from *Imposter Syndrome*, where you think that your words aren't good enough, aren't relevant enough that people will want to pay money for them. Or that whatever success you've had came to you through blind luck and not because of your own skill.

I'm going to be a little rude, but you need to get over yourself, princess. And don't tell me that everyone suffers from it, because that's a crock of shit. Lots of professionals I know can barely spell the word. Doubt is fine. Get over that, too. If you are any good as writer, people will want to read your books. If you truly are an imposter, why the hell are you bothering people? Stop this and go find something that makes you happy. It's better than punishing yourself (and everyone else).

I'd rather you be happy as an artist than a miserable SOB driving the professionals nuts by whining at them all the time. Grow up and put on your big-boy pants. This is a book for professionals and either you are one, or you are not. Imposters shouldn't be here, so stop being one, or stop pretending to be a writer.

QUESTION: *Do you deserve to be here?* Simple as that. If you do, then let's get to work making your Author Brand look good so you can sell some books.

Speed

Now we're getting down to that thing that separates TradPub from Indie. In the old days, you were generally allowed to publish one book per year. That's why folks crossed genre and created new pennames, so they could perhaps publish a romance, a fantasy, and a mystery all in the same year.

The world has changed.

There are no gatekeepers telling you that you have to spend an entire year on one novel. That you should redraft it half a dozen times before its "ready" like some MFA programs seem intent on teaching folks. When you do that, chances are you are stripping out all the raw emotions and *Voice* that made it good in the first place. The Fifth Draft might be utter perfection filled with pretty words, and boring as shit because you made all the characters vanilla. I'll even be so rude as to suggest that a good copy edit on your first draft would probably make a better book than your fifth draft ended up being.

But MFA programs teach you to "craft" your words. The secret? Teachers don't want to read lots of stuff for grading, so they want you to write slow. They even go so far as to suggest that anyone writing fast must be turning out crap.

Given some of the things they put out, I could see where they would assume that everyone else writes like they do. Crap. Ask your MFA professor how many novels he or she has written. Or, better, how much money they made from their books last year. That's the real measure for us professionals.

I support myself on my writing. No day job. Most of the TradPub folks I know can't say that. Can't even pretend to be remotely close to supporting a household on their writing. (Having a supportive spouse who works to pay the bills doesn't count. When you can cause them to retire to support you, then you are winning.)

Speed is critical in the new, Indie world, because readers want to read books. Lots of books. Constantly. If they like you, they will buy all your books. If you put out one book per year, they will forget about you by then, or just won't pay that much attention. You're back to square one, and every reader is a new reader at that point.

There are folks that make me look like an absolute, bloody piker, and I'm writing at Pulp Speed One (1,000,000 word/year) and change. (Technically, paced at Pulp Two, which is 100,000 words per month, but we'll keep the math simple.) I think my sister in law is writing something like 5-7,000 words per day, 6-7 days per week right now. Lots of bloody words. She's that good. And that focused on her craft. Her novels sell lots.

Readers want to finish something and buy the next. And the next. And the next.

Fast does not mean crap. I'll put my storytelling up against anyone's. There are writers with a better craft at pretty words, but your one novel is not twenty times better than the twenty I plan to write this year.

If you wish to be successful today (TODAY mind you), the formula involves putting out more product. How much is up to you. What is the pace you can sustain and not burn out?

We generally use 1,000 words/hour as a gauge when a professional sits down to write. If you are working for 3-4 hours, you should have 3-4,000 words. Five days per week, that's 15-20,000 words. Or a novel about every three weeks.

Go back and read that sentence again.

What is your writing pace?

Okay, I promised that this would be for Publishers, so I'll leave off talking to the writers. Except that as a publisher, you need to understand your author's *Brand*. If they are a slow writer and nothing will ever change that, you have a different approach than someone dropping 1-2 novels every month, like me.

RULE: ONE SIZE DOES NOT FIT ALL.

From a marketing standpoint, writing quickly gives you options. I can write an entire series of science fiction books, say five of them, get them First Readered, copy edited, and ready to drop on a short schedule, because I'm working that far ahead and that fast at putting out product.

Write/Release Versus Rapid Release

There might be a method to my madness here. Or a madness to my method. Whatever.

There are two ways you can approach publishing your author's books. If they write slowly, releasing a book as quickly as you can get it through the pipeline (edits, cover, blurb, etc.) and into your reader's hands might be your best way to maintain mindshare with your readers.

When she writes faster, you (the publisher) can get all of the books in hand, and prepare a Series marketing plan that will build up enthusiasm and sales better and more coherently by dropping them in short order, with the pre-order for the next book already up before the current books goes live and ad campaigns teed up. Romance writers are the masters of this field, sometimes publishing an entire series all at once, so that readers can just binge on them and drive sales through the roof one month.

I don't do that, but that's because I have a different kind of career plan, and work hard to take advantage of the Amazon Pulses, which we'll talk about in a later chapter. Instead, I publish at least one thing on the 10th of every month. Some months that will be one novel. Others I might drop several shorter pieces. I also edit and publish a science fiction magazine (Boundary Shock Quarterly, www.boundaryshockquarterly.com) so I've usually got a new issue dropping in Jan, Apr, Jul, and Oct. That's on top of the novels.

How fast will your author generate product? Let that drive your release schedule planning and your sanity, but understand that these days (and it will probably change at some point), faster writers generating more product are the best way to make good money.

Your best advertising is always to write the next book. I just dropped book seven in the Jessica Keller series (***St. Legier***, came out Dec 2018), and people see ads for that novel, so they look, bounce back, and buy book one (***Auberon***) to read the whole series and catch up. This is passive marketing, but it works.

Active Versus Passive?

There are two sets of ways you market. (Much of this is covered in ***Business for Breakfast: The Beginning Professional Publisher.***)

Active marketing involves running advertisements on social media or publisher websites. It is you walking into a local bookstore to try to get them to order and carry your book. It is ACTIVE. The Hustle. You, being active. Talking to people, or at least having to be involved in things. Yuck.

Passive marketing covers all the little things you do once and let them set. The place I hope you will start out, dipping your toes and figuring out what works for you. Examples include a cover that hits genre hard (whatever your genre is) and communicates to the potential buyer exactly what to expect for tone. It builds excitement to buy your books. Blurbs that tell them what story to expect, so you better have a good one, and it better accurately prepare them.

Take a blurbs class sometime, because until you do, you are writing bad blurbs. (WMG Publishing offers a good one. So do others.) Its all ad copy, so learn how to do it correctly. Joseph Sugarman is a really good place to start. It is an old book, but the concepts have not changed, because he's working on human psychology.

Passive marketing does not take up a lot of your time. You do it once and then leave it until you have a reason to change something. Those are the things you should concentrate on at the beginning, for that reason. WIBBOW.

Wide Versus Narrow

One other topic I want to touch, before we start to get into the gritty details of things, involves your decision whether you want to be widely distributed or narrow. In specific terms, do you want to be exclusive with one distributor, or available anywhere?

Amazon (currently) has Kindle Unlimited (KU), which is a subscription service where a reader can sign up and can read anything that they want (that is itself exclusive in KU) for a single fee. For fast readers, it is the greatest deal you can get, but there are problems. Only those books that are exclusive to Amazon can be in KU. Any fans the writer might have on other platforms cannot read it, and that might piss them off.

As a personal example, I used to listen to country music (yeah, I know). Garth Brooks, when he was the biggest thing on the planet, released an album that was a Walmart Exclusive, meaning you could only buy it at Walmart. I don't shop there. But by doing this, he pissed me off so much that I still don't own that album, and I could not tell you if he ever released another album after that because I stopped being a fan of his over it. And that's maybe twenty or more years ago now.

Studies have shown that you can make good money in KU, but that your fans there will not come out of KU to read anything else you publish elsewhere. They want all the books they can gorge on for that one, low price, rather than buying your entire catalog.

In fact, I know a lot of people who are now trapped in KU, because they like the money (which appears to be receding, month over month) and now have to figure out how to go wide and recreate their fan base from scratch, with people who have never heard of them. Think back to multiple pennames and having to start over each time. Those writers won't do it in a month. They might not do it in a year. They might never do it.

Is the draw of fast, easy money worth it to you? Versus distributing your books on many platforms and building a more organic fanbase?

Examples to consider include Barnes & Noble (no, they're not dead yet), Apple Books (what used to be iTunes/iBooks), Kobo (we'll go into more detail later) and several others. You don't need to know them all, as we'll talk later about a service called D2D ("Draft To Digital") that exists to get your ebooks into a wide variety of smaller venues, especially the newer ones that are popping up all the time. There is also Google Play, but I and others have had issues there. I won't ever put my books up on their site.

You will need to make that determination for yourself. My job here is to lay out as much information as I can, including making my biases obvious, so you can make a good decision, and hopefully jumpstart your career.

With me so far?

Okay, let's get into details and checklists.

Your Website

Narrowcasting

I'm going to start out with a new term I learned from some major players in 2018 when they let me sneak into the room and hide in the corner. **Narrowcasting**. It has massive implications for your career over the next 3-5 years, and maybe the next decade or more, so you need to understand what it is and how to work with it.

In the old days, broadcasting meant just that, sending a radio (and later television) signal out and trying to gather the broadest amount of listeners. You went wide, so everyone might tune in. As a result, you frequently had to tack to the middle of the road in nearly all things cultural, so as to not offend either end of the listener spectrum. Think Walter Cronkite giving you the news of the whole nation, with no particular political slant, as opposed to the vast majority of British newspapers.

Back when there were basically three choices on TV, you had to compete with the other two for the most viewers, so that you could command the most ad dollars from the people paying money to put their commercials on any given show.

The world has changed.

Cable television eventually exploded the old model, just like

FM did to radio, because there were now so many other places to compete. As a result, a brand (see? There's that word again) could be successfully built around a niche. (Think your voice and your books, compared to the Classic Rock or Classical music station.) You could find the cable station doing the thing you wanted to watch, rather than having to settle for whatever was on the big three. Similarly, the world wide web let someone put up a fan page for a single thing and interact with other people with the same interests. *Otaku*. Hobbies are like that.

So now let's look at what happened *after* everyone had their own web site. Social Media came along, as a way to "aggregate" people back into a single place. (Many of you will think of Facebook, but before that there was MySpace, or AOL, or others. Understand that things change, and nobody has a MySpace page anymore. Or just a few of you.)

Similarly, the eventual response to all the crap on cable was to cut the cord and sign up for television aggregator services like Netflix, Hulu, or others, where you could watch just the things you wanted to, and not pay a stupid amount of money for the rest.

We're at the beginning of 2019 as I write this. Disney has removed all of their content from those middlemen (Netflix, Hulu, etc.) because they are supposedly going to launch their own Disney-branded channel (possibly before you actually read these words), and that will be the only place you can watch their shows and movies. CBS has several new Star Trek shows going right now, but you have to sign up for their service, because it is exclusive. (Remember me talking about the exclusivity trap earlier with Garth Brooks? I haven't watched the new shows. And probably won't, any time soon. Maybe one of these days when I can buy them on disk or some such.)

We are moving out of broadcasting, where there was one place to get all your news or entertainment, and into narrowcasting, where you have to go to different places to find your fix. Some of you are old enough to remember rss feeds, so bloody important because it was such a pain in the ass to keep track of everything and go all those places to find your news.

My personal theory is that Facebook is already in the process of turning into MySpace, for a variety of reasons. There will always be a need for some manner of social media, so that people can keep track of old friends or coworkers, but the drive to spend time there will go down. The numbers are supporting it. People are moving away from THAT social media platform, but there is not a single one that replaces it. Wattpad. Pinterest. YouTube. Discord. Snapchat. Etc. My bet is something nobody has even heard of yet.

The world is fragmenting. It will come back together at some future point, but nobody knows when, and I'm pretty sure that the platform the replaces it hasn't even been built yet.

You, the author the brand, need to prepare for a fragmented world, for the simple reason that you need to be everywhere at once, in order to be discoverable by your fans.

In a narrowcasting world, discoverability becomes harder, because you can't just run some Facebooks ads and pull in lots of folks. Things like that will work less and less over time. Already are. All those weekly email things where people sign up to maybe win a bunch of ebooks will work well for a short period of time, and then fade. They do that.

Your Website

Which brings me to your personal website. This is the place you own and control. (You must own it and control it, Bubbles.) When Myspace went away, all your fans went away with it, because that company owned the connection, not you. The same will occur on Facebook (FB). And everywhere else.

You need to be someplace that will not be shut down. Where you can't be evicted without cause (anybody here have a Tumblr account that they deleted? Anybody get put into FB timeout for advertising?). This is the place where you control the horizontal and the vertical. I know a bunch of old farts that suddenly lost everything a few years ago because the website and email address they had been using for **decades** was on someone else's server and dime, and that company went bankrupt. They lost twenty or thirty years' worth of email and old things, because it wasn't theirs to begin with.

You must have your own personal website.

I cannot stress that fact hard enough or loud enough. All of your marketing, active and passive, will exist to drive fans to that place. Go find an easy to remember (and SPELL) web domain and purchase it. Preferably one that includes your name (or penname, but something that a search engine will find you with.) Put a reminder in to keep the registration up to date, or set the system to auto-renew itself for you. They'll do that. (I say easy to spell url because I'm working with a young author who has an email address that is quite easy to remember, and almost impossible to spell, because she went phonetic. Cute, but counter-productive. Make it easy for your fans. I'll explain why in greater detail later.)

As a quick note, most of the reputable services will let you register your domain, and put a website on it, for a single, low cost per year. If you attach it to a credit card, you can also turn on annual renewal as well, so you don't lose it accidentally. As of now, the whole package: hosting, url registration, privacy feature should run you around $180 per year. Sub-domains, if you have them, should be much cheaper individually and one should be included in that price, depending. Fabulous Publisher Babe™ tells me that a Publisher site and an author-name-subdomain are the most effective set-up here, but we're not going to deep dive and confuse you today. Just understand that there are folks out there you can bribe with food or wine to help with those questions, when you get there.

My world (www.blazeward.com) is [CURRENTLY] hosted on Bluehost, (though according to Fabulous Publisher Babe™ that will change soon) and is running the following technical tools: Wordpress, Jetpack, Mooberry Book Manager, Wordfence Security. As an author, there are other things you can do, but understand that I'm exceedingly lazy, and want this to just work without having to do maintenance more than maybe monthly.

Okay, while we're on the topic, when you get your domain, set up email on it and stop using your yahoo, aol, or gmail email account for professional business. I still have a Hotmail account that's almost twenty years old, but that's for spam and old stuff. Business is on my bw.com email.

I hope you were already aware of all the AI tools that Google (and those other places) uses to scan each gmail that you send, so they can advertise to you, or sell that information to someone else that wants to advertise to you. Your private email is not private. If you aren't paying for the product, you ARE the product, and they need to monetize you.

Okay, have I hammered it home enough? There are people out there who can help you set up your website, and good ones that won't change an arm and a leg. If you get a quote for more than $500, you need to step back and have them show you the other sites that they have done and watch how those leave you gasping with awesomeness. Or those people are pulling a fast one on you.

Also, consider trading favors with people you know who do set up websites. My wife frequently works for good dinners, with people she likes, like my cousin, who is also a writer. There's absolutely something you can trade. Get creative and weird. You are an artist, after all.

Page One

The landing page (home page) of your website needs to be static. No flashing lights and dancing girls. A welcome note, with a few paragraphs about what just came out, what's coming out next, and a bunch of tabs or obvious links to other things farther in. That's it. Let your readers/fans get the most important information immediately, and then let them dive deeper into the site to find other things.

Newsletter signup

I'll touch more on newsletters as things later, but make sure that there is a very obvious place on Page One where a new fan can quickly and easily sign up for your newsletter. For me, that's a link off to the side of the main page, and it's also in my author bio in a number of places, at the very top. Plus, there's a popup (though not an obnoxious one.)

When you get people signed up for your newsletter, do not spam them with crap. Do not EVER sell or share their email address with someone else. And make it clear that you will carry out that goal. Gmail sells my address to anyone and everyone who will give them money. I almost never actually look at my gmail account anymore, due to all the spam and crap it gets.

The EASIEST way for fans to keep track of you is a periodic newsletter, so make it easy for them to get wrapped up into your world.

Another thing, and it is really more of an intermediate task, so you can skip it for now, but remember to come back to it, is what they call auto-responders. The tools are rather easy today for you to be able to immediately send someone a note when they sign up for your newsletter saying something along the lines of "Thanks for signing up for my newsletter. Here's what to expect…".

In a more advanced book later, we'll go into greater detail about layering auto-responders, but that's way more than you need to worry about today. My suggestion would be go read **Newsletter Ninja** by Tammi Labrecque and maybe take her class. Fabulous Publisher Babe™ did and highly recommends it. We're still implementing everything for me as I write this. I can't give you a higher recommendation than that.

Blog

You need a blog. I'm sorry, but this is like the Imposter Syndrome discussion earlier. You will need to come to grips with it and get over yourself. You are a writer, so people want to hear what you have to say, and not just in your books. They want the unvarnished you. You: the author, the brand. That includes a blog.

And it should be more than "here's the inspiration behind story X." That can be a useful thing to do, but you will need more if you want to engage people.

Why? Because you will need to blog regularly. I know people who are daily. Others aim for weekly. But you need to put things out there. They don't have to be earth-shaking. I just wrote a note this week about the milestone of finishing my twenty-fifth novel, and how weird that felt. Another recent one was trying to get all my fans to go over and sign up for Daniel Keys Moran's new Patreon (www.patreon.com/fatsam) so we could convince Dan that he could make a nice living from books, and that he would write more of the Continuing Times books he promised me thirty years ago. (Blackmail is such an ugly term…)

The goal is with blogging is to put your words out there where your fans can read them and get to know you better. I count all of my blogs as sellable words each month, because they are part of the active marketing of me, even though they are kinda passive.

Your blog should not show up on Page One. Have a link to it for fans to read when they arrive. Most likely, they'll come in from somewhere else directly, and go straight to that page to read. They can also usually sign up so that every time you write a blog, it will show up in their email inbox as a reminder that you exist and you're awesome. Take advantage of that.

But at the same time, make sure you take advantage of the outward feeds. Every time I blog, it automatically feeds to my Facebook author/fan page, my Amazon author page, my Goodreads page, and a few other places. Write once, appear everywhere. And every one of those outbound links pulls readers back into my website, where they look around and maybe go buy other books, because they missed one. (I know, it happens.)

Content: Books

This is the passive marketing part of your website, where the blog and the newsletter are semi-active. There is a product called Mooberry Books Manager that lets you have an individual page for every book (novel or short), with links to as many vendors as you put in. (I cheat and bounce things over to Knotted Road Press where my wife/boss already does this, so I don't have to do it twice. Here you go: http://knottedroadpress.com/browse-krp-books/by-author-blaze-ward/).

Additionally, Mooberry lets you show things in series. I write in series, so it is helpful if someone can go one place and get the list they need.

I also have a page on my own site where things are organized into genre and extended universe, because the Alexandria Station books are kinda messy, if you wander in sideways and don't have context. (And yes, I just spent an hour going over everything when I realized I had gotten behind and it wasn't fully up to date.)

Once you have the people on your website, the goal is to make everything sticky. Keep them engaged here. If they wander somewhere else, you might not get them back, unless the place they go is to buy more of your books.

The Tip Jar

I have a tip jar on the side of my website. Shows up on a sidebar on all the pages, I think, based on the theme I'm using. Nothing special to it. Here's the actual language I use, so you can steal it later (but change the link, unless you want me getting all your money).

"If you feel like you learned something, or I made you smile, or you just enjoyed yourself here, feel free to leave a tip! Click paypal.me/BlazeWard to go to PayPal."

Occasionally, people drop $5 in it with a note to go get coffee, because they so enjoyed the book they just read. That's over the price they paid to buy it. It happens. And I have one superfan who has dropped off coffee money more than once, because I made him laugh, or smile, or something. One more way for fans to show their appreciation.

As my wife and I remind each other, everything we do in Indie Publishing generates nickels. "**But them nickels spend.**"

The Newsletter

Okay, so we've got your website in good enough shape now that someone accidentally wandering along can find what they need with a minimum of fuss. They can follow your blog on whatever platform they consume those things on. Marvelous. That part is the passive marketing of you. (Yes, blogging is kinda active, but we're about to talk about active marketing, so you'll see the difference shortly, I hope.)

The best suggestions I have seen for newsletters from you: the author, the brand, seem to rotate around doing something monthly. You can do bi-weekly, but in that case, you should probably set up two different styles of writing and address things two different ways. And it's more work, so let's just have a single, monthly newsletter.

I drop a new title on the 10th of every month, and aim to get the newsletter out around the 15th. So it makes sense that my monthly newsletter covers what just came out, and what's coming next. Nothing more than that. Links to both and quick descriptions. If the reader likes you enough to be a fan, chances are they're already signed up for the preorders, so you don't need to hard sell here.

I also own six acres of trees and swamp out southeast of Seattle past the first ridge of the Cascade Mountains, so I frequently mention whatever it is I'm doing recently. Last summer, we stripped the pumphouse roof down to the studs and put a new one on, plus stripping the walls and putting up new siding. I also grow lots of fruit, so I jar things regularly in the summer, and talk about that.

Me.

I'm a person, like you (I hope you qualify), and your fans want to know who you are. It's okay to talk about your cats in your newsletter, because that might be part of who you are. Find your own balance of sharing, but that will create warmer, richer, deeper relationships with folks you are asking to give you money. I have more than one fan who come to the big, annual events the wife and I hold, coming across country at their own expense, because we've become friends. Amazing things happen when you make friends out of fans. Welcome it.

But keep the hard sell soft. *Here's the latest. Did you miss? This crazy thing happened to me the other day.* Another thing you can research is what's called Content Marketing. These are more advanced techniques that people like **Joanna Penn** (https://www.thecreativepenn.com/) uses to build up very deep relationships with her fans, by sharing interesting web links to things related to her stories, or things she came across in her research that she thought people who like her books might enjoy reading. She's a lovely lady, much fun to listen to, and can teach us all a great deal about these sorts of things.

THERE YOU HAVE IT. Website fundamentals. Own your content so it never goes away. Keep it simple and well organized. Keep it up to date. Don't spend a lot of time on it, but don't let it go so stale that it still mentions a new book that's going to come out in 2016. (Yes, I saw that author page not too long ago and chewed his ass about it.)

Everything else you do is going to be designed to drive all web traffic here. Not to your Social Media page (your Myspace or AOL still active?). We want people coming to **you.com** for their fix.

In the Narrowcasting world, we don't want to have to reinvent ourselves on every platform. Bring them here and you also control the message. I hate to tell you how many of my friends have gotten timeouts on FB for doing their hard hustle so much that the machines objected and shut them down for 7 or 30 days.

Bring them to someplace you control instead.

Know What You Write

Genre

I gotta spend time here because I'm constantly amazed that most authors have no clue how to identify the genre of the story they have just written. Granted, I have an unfair advantage, but still.

I used to write stage plays and screenplays. (None of them ever got made into movies, but that's a different story.) In that field, you must absolutely know your genre going in. That meant that I knew I was writing X type of story before I ever created characters. I had to know the ten rules of that genre. I had to nail nine of them perfectly, just so I could step sideways and do something weird with the tenth. I had an exact length of story I could tell. (90-120 pages, formatted in a unalterably-specific style. Period.)

You (the writer part of the equation) have just written something. What genre category is it in?

Erotica trumps everything else. If it's of an adult, explicit style, that's where it's going. You don't get to argue with me on that, because the Amazon machines will win anyway.

Romance trumps next. And you better hit every damned one of the romance rules if you do intend to call it a romance. If you don't hit them all, it is not a romance, but something else and you can market it with romantic elements. Romance readers are savage when angered. Don't mess with them.

Science fiction comes next. If the story has aliens, I don't care that it is a mystery. It will get filed on the SF shelf.

Are you beginning to see pattern here?

Readers are on rails. Go take your publisher hat off for a second and put on your **reader** hat. Now pretend to walk into your favorite book store and tell me what section you immediately end up facing. See? Rails.

You end up looking at a specific shelf, based on the genre you prefer. Sometimes, a specific author or letter of the alphabet, if you're like me. If you can control your genre going into the story, like I can, all the better for the publisher to know how to cover, blurb, and market it.

Mystery readers do not generally read science fiction. They consider it too low brow for them, even if it is a good mystery. SciFi readers are more forgiving, and are more likely to follow you if you suddenly put out a mystery or thriller. If you try to sell a SF mystery as Mystery, you better make damned clear (cover, blurb, etc.) that they are dealing with SF, or they'll burn you, much like romance readers.

I'm not telling you to write in clearly demarcated categories. I am telling you as a publisher that you must understand how genre works, so that you get your book in front of the right readers. And don't try to fake it. You will lose, and end up alienating the very fans you need.

Exception: YA

So now we need to talk about a couple of exceptions to the rules of genre. YA, short for Young Adult Fiction, is a special thing. They can be fantasy, urban fantasy, science fiction, or post-apocalyptic in style, but the fact that they meet the rules for YA trumps everything else and they go on those shelves. Harry Potter, The Hunger Games, and The Maze Runner are all in the YA category, despite being so radically different in the places they go and the worlds they describe.

You can't change those rules, so don't try. If you have a legitimate YA novel, good for you, because that's still a powerful category for selling books today, although I suspect that those days are numbered. The category won't go away, but it will drop back down to what it was twenty-five years ago, before JK Rowling changed the world. You'll still sell in it, but there will probably just be fewer readers interested.

Exception: Westerns

I catch hell occasionally for pointing out that Western is not a true genre, like fantasy or mystery or science fiction. It is a place. (And a bookshelf all by itself, which is why we're having this conversation.) 19th Century United States of America. Generally west of St. Louis, Missouri. Usually in the tighter time category of 1870-1890.

Cowboys. Maybe the Indian Wars. Post Civil War.

If you write a cowboy story, chances are it is getting filed with all the rest of the Westerns. It can be a coming of age story. A bank robbery caper. A mystery. Doesn't matter. You're getting filed with the cowboys.

Until the mid-Twentieth Century, cowboy books were a huge genre. I saw a stat recently breaking down Hollywood (read: US) movies by genre, every year after 1918. Westerns utterly dominated, until they fell off a cliff in about 1955. (I'm guessing Science Fiction and Rock and Roll ate them.) There was a comeback from about 1965-1975. Then nothing. Less than one percent of movies released each year today.

Gone. Just like that.

Western literature as a genre did much the same thing. There are still writers. There are readers. But they are a MUCH smaller cadre of people and dollars than they used to be.

Now, mind you, Romance with a wild west theme still generally gets filed in Romance, and seems to do well over there, but that's Romance, and it trumps if you go there. You must commit to being a romance writer, understand your craft and the rules of your sub-sub-subgenre, and then nail them with a twenty pound maul. But you can do it.

But if you write a basic western bank robbery story, what a modern reader might call a caper if it occurred in the present day, it's still a western.

I don't make these rules. You won't break them, unless you get really lucky perhaps, maybe by putting out Weird West and Steampunk, which move you sideways just enough sideways to fall under science fiction instead. But even then, they are small categories within the overall realm of SF, so prepare to not necessarily make a lot of money there either. And that category (Steampunk/Weird West) seems to be fading from the heights it hit a decade or two ago.

OKAY, I hope that helps you understand something important about genre. The writer doesn't have to know a damned thing, and she can keep on putting out whatever stories set her heart on fire. But the publisher damned sure better understand how to get that story onto the right shelf, so the right fans will find it.

Once you have a fan base, they are more likely to follow you, even if you stray from the thing that made them fall in love with you, but most readers are on rails. They walk into the bookstore and immediately go to the Romance section. Or Mystery. Thriller. SFF. Make sure your covers and blurbs silently convey genre, so that the reader can decide if they want to cross over with you. Many will, if you are a good brand, but not always.

Mystery, thriller, and romance tend to be isolated. If readers to cross over, Science Fiction/Fantasy seems to be the one place where they might go. And SFF fans will be more forgiving to cross back into one of those.

Again, you are the brand.

Organizing Your Work

I wrote a blog recently (Title: "Do you want to be famous or rich?") where I laid out four steps that have been extremely successful for me and a number of other authors working today. We're going to revisit them today, because in all honesty, that blog post is about half of what inspired this book.

I call the path Story, Novel, Series, EU.

I can't help you write better stories. (Technically, I can, with my two Business For Breakfast books: *The Beginning Professional Storyteller* and *The Three Act Structure for Professional Writers*, depending on the technical level of your craft.) My suggestion is that you learn to write better first drafts. I start each morning by rereading what I wrote yesterday, and fixing typos and missing words. There is no rewriting, unless I read a sentence and even I can't figure out what I was trying to say. Call it 15-30 minutes at most getting yesterday's work out of the way and clean. Then I start writing today's words.

When I get to the end of the novel, the first drafts are extremely clean. I put them aside for a week or a month and do other things, and then come back, do one hard pass to fix typos, and send it off to the First Readers. I take their corrections somewhere around 90-95% of the time (I have good people). Send it off to the Publisher. Write the next story better.

You will not write twenty novels in a year if you spend hours agonizing over each sentence and revising it seventeen times. Learn to write your draft quickly, and do it clean and unbroken, so you can move on.

Next, you are going to need to write novels. In the old days, a newbie learned her craft by writing short fiction of progressively higher quality, eventually getting it placed into the major genre magazines and making a name for herself, possibly winning awards. Some folks even managed to make a living at short fiction in the old days, but I've already done the math in *Business of Breakfast: Writing At Pulp Speed*, so I don't feel like revisiting it here. You can't make a living today.

Eventually, our fearless author would make a good name for

herself and reach that stage where she considered her craft good enough that she could start writing a novel and eventually shop it to an agent.

There are no more agents. None worth a damn, anyway. If that's the career path you envision, why are you even this deep into this book?

But you do need to learn to write novels. Can't stress that enough. That's what the reader wants. Depending on your genre, they might be 50,000 words, and they might be 250,000. Go look at the recent best sellers in your sub-sub-genre category and you'll quickly get a feel for what you need to be doing by dead weight.

You will not make money at shorter lengths. (And yes, I managed to do that, but I'm still not sure what caused a novella series, each book 24-32k, to spike so hard on the sales that I made major Amazon bestseller lists. The Amazon Magic Machine picked my name out of a hat one day. Don't rely on it. I don't.)

So, now that you are writing longer and committing novels instead of short stories, we need to talk about series work. Television has trained the viewer to expect one long, ongoing story that spans seasons and perhaps entire shows. Gone are the days when every week was entirely self-contained and complete, what many shows called "Monster of the Week." Now you have arcs. Readers want the same thing.

That translates into series. And I don't mean trilogies, although that can kind of work. A trilogy is a thing that has a beginning, a middle, and an end. Three Acts, that follow certain storytelling rules. When you have a series, your characters are continuing, and the story might just keep running.

The Jessica Keller Chronicles ends at nine core novels, plus a side trilogy and two unrelated novellas. Fans want to keep coming back to the same friends and see how their lives change. Watch them grow and mature. See some of them die off. See others suddenly spurt to prominence. Evolution.

These days, many readers won't even touch a series until they know that it is done, or at least deep enough into it that the author should finish it. TradPub burned them so badly by publishing what was obviously a Book One, but not following through on Two and Three, so nobody ever found out how the story ended. The reader does not want to get emotionally attached to a character until they know that the relationship will continue.

So you need to learn to write your novels in series. I have several. My personal series definition is a minimum of five novels (around 45-50,000 words each) worth of material, or around 225-250,000 words, give or take. Long enough to do something big, but short enough that I can finish the series off and go on to something else before I burn myself out or get bored writing it. I frequently also bring a series to a resting point without "finishing" it, so I can start up again. The first eight of The Science Officer novellas I consider Season One, because I plan to come back and start writing Season Two in 2019. And they'll probably end up being short novels instead of long novellas.

Finally, there is the Extended Universe. My Alexandria Station stories are a great example. As of today (Jan 2019): 9 Javier Aritza novellas (one unpublished); 13 Jessica Keller books in various flavors and lengths; 3 Doyle Iwakuma; 2 Handsome Rob; 1 Henri Baudin; 1 Lansdowne.

So far.

Let me repeat that: **SO FAR**.

29 stories. All one universe. Suvi ties the whole thing together by appearing in many of them.

I plan to write more Javier and Handsome Rob this year. I still owe everyone two more Henri and the other two Lansdowne. I want to tell Olivier's story. Plus I intentionally left myself holes into which I could do other things. Jean-Pierre. Wilhelmina. MORE.

Fans already know the universe, so much of the world-building can be minimized, leaving me more space for story.

And all sorts of Easter Eggs I can bury, to reward the ones that have read everything else.

As you'll note here, the goal of everything we are doing, from both an active and passive marketing standpoint, is to get your fans [more] engaged. Make them happy. They want to give you money. They do that by buying your books and telling their friends. Everybody wins.

Everything you do needs to be driven by that central equation.

Amazonia and Friends

WE'RE GOING to talk about the nine hundred pound gorilla first, because in North America, they are the single biggest mover of books. Barnes & Noble has been death-spiraling for a long time, and are too intimately intertwined with TradPub to really matter to those of us in Indie.

A personal example for you to chew on: In 2017 (I haven't done the 2018 numbers yet), I sold 92 paper books, and little over 32,000 ebooks. Read that math again. Less than one tenth of one percent of my sales were paper. And I had a fantastically nice year. But I'm not in B&N on any shelf. I'm in their catalog, so someone could order my books, but nobody does. In 2019, I'm actually going to experiment with some changes to see if I can generate more paper sales, but I'm never going to rely on them, and they won't make me rich.

The company I give more attention to than B&N is Kobo (www.kobo.com), an ebook-only distributor that started in Canada and is slowly expanding into the rest of the planet, one country at a time. They are competitive with Amazon in many places, and I have fans in strange lands. (They have a sales map that's utterly cool, and one of the easiest interfaces to upload books I have found.) But Amazon owns the US market, and is a major presence in Canada. It you are wanting to make money, you need to be cognizant of what they do, and how they do it.

For most readers in the US (and let's expand that to the English-dominant countries by including Canada, Great Britain, Australia, and New Zealand where I have had good sales experience) Amazon is a big chunk of their income. Most authors are trying to reduce that number, and there are number of ways to do it, but let's get you big and rich before we move on to those strategies.

Another couple of places I want to mention while we're here are Apple Books and Google Play. Apple Books is a closed ecosystem, what we used to call a "walled garden," where you can only put your books up if you have a Mac-based computer, and only find those books from a Mac browser. I don't go direct to them, but use D2D as a service, even though we have Macs, just because their upload system is painful to use, non-intuitive, and drives me crazy. They don't seem to want to compete with Amazon the way Kobo does.

Google Play I will leave to the imagination. I won't ever put my books up there. Others have done so and seem to do well. Lucky them.

Moving on…

The Pulse

I am given to understand, by hints dropped by Amazon representatives that did not violate NDAs, that Amazon's machine intelligences have a set of publishing pulses that they recognize. These occur at 30, 60, and perhaps 90 days.

To put that in English, if you publish something about every thirty days (the same day every month is apparently good enough), the machines apparently reward you in various ways. Better placements in also-boughts. Better suggestions. Etc. The same apparently works if you drop something every sixty days. We're still not sure how well the ninety day thing works, but most of us are on a faster pulse anyway.

RULE OF PUBLISHERS: *Make sure you have claimed*

your *Amazon Author page. Put a good bio on it, and include a link to sign up for you author's newsletter at the top, before the bio parts.*

ANOTHER RULE: *Do not talk about your cats in your author bio. Talk about your books, your series, and any awards you have won.*

ANOTHER RULE: *Make sure you are following yourself on Amazon.* Can't stress that enough, because you need to see what your fans see, in case you need to fix something.

What frequently happens is that Amazon sends me an email that says that Blaze Ward has a new book up for pre-order, with a link to it for the fans to immediately jump on. Other times, I get an email that says Blaze Ward's new book has been published. Or a reminder two to six weeks later: Did you miss Blaze Ward's book?

They don't all happen each month, but I usually get one of them with some regularity.

This is Amazon doing the active marketing for you. FOR YOU. You aren't sending emails to people. Amazon is. It costs you nothing but a brief set-up. If they won't share with you the names and email addresses of the people they ping, those people are still getting a notice to spend money on you. I just got one this morning for my wife, also a writer.

This is also why the newsletter signup link needs to be at the top of your bio, because on the current Amazon Author Page interface, that puts it right below the [Follow This Author] button. Good placement for you to take advantage of.

I am not aware of something similar that Kobo or B&N do, to say nothing of the "smaller" publishers out there. Amazon does it, and does it for free, as long as you publish something regularly. Let them work for you. Others, like Bookbud sort of do as well, at least today.

This circles us back to fast writers and one of their advantages. I can write a whole series, and then drop them month over month, with pre-orders already live for the next book. Amazon likes that.

If you are a slower writer, do not despair. I also have short story series I have written. All the 'bot cares about is that I published something on the 10th, not the length. If you are still working on writing faster, write a bunch of short stories some month, and sit on them, parceling them out each month to get/keep the pulse going. Alternatively, I taught myself how to stop in the middle of a novel, pivot and write a short story, and then get back into the novel without missing a beat, just to keep the 30-Day pulse going. You can do the same.

Claiming Your Books

Once you have set up your Amazon Author page, and put a PROFESSIONAL bio on it (repeating here: nothing about your cats, unless you write Cat Cozies and maybe not even then.), then you need to log in to Amazon's Author Central and claim your books. (As I write this, the url is https://authorcentral.amazon.com but that might change without notice, so don't just trust me here.)

Every time you publish something, or put a book up for pre-order, claim it on Author Central a day later, so that it shows up under your name, and the 'bots know it is your book, so they can start sending out the marketing emails for you. When you fans search for you, they can then see ALL your books.

Amazon owns this data, and there's nothing we can do about that, but make it easier for people to find you, your books, and your website.

Jeff Bezos, Founder of Amazon (and current CEO as I write these words.) wants to win. Period. Whatever market sector he goes into, he has a plan, a goal, and a definition of success that does not involve being a distant third to other folks. He wants to win.

The man functionally invented Indie Publishing as we know it. Others might have done things first, but he made it possible and easy for authors to publish ebooks, and for readers to find and buy them.

He created my lifestyle, and everyone else has spent twenty years either trying to play catch-up, or slowly being eaten by the man. If you suffer from *Amazon Derangement Syndrome*, you need to get over it, because Jeff wants to win, and will do whatever he needs to do to take down everyone else (legally, as far as I know). He's eaten TradPub, like a snake digesting a half-dozen stupid, fat rabbits. Everyone else is just trying to keep up with him, and you can let him do a lot of the work for you. He will help you sell a crapton of books, if you let him.

On the flip side, my experience with the Google's Books option was so bad that I took everything down and will never put my stuff up there for sale again, at least until the people in charge have cleaned out all the fraud that seemed to be rampant. I've heard from others that it has "gotten better" but not great. (I bought my own book, just see how it worked on their site, and it has never shown up as a sale, and I've never gotten paid a royalty for it. Never. Years. You do the math. Other places might call that fraud.)

Kobo (www.kobo.com) on the other hand is a fantastic competitor for Amazon in the ebook space. They recently signed a deal with Walmart to sell ebooks there, because Walmart has finally woken up to the competition and the need to do things to compete with Amazon in the book categories. We all win, both as authors and consumers, from such competition. You can go to Walmart's website to get ebooks and Kobo will fulfill it for you, so ALL of Kobo's catalog is available.

My only issue with Kobo (literally, I love those folks) is that Science Fiction represents such a tiny fraction of their overall sales that I don't have a large pool of readers to attract in the first place, outside of whatever Walmart might bring to North America. Romance, Mystery, and Thriller (if I remember correctly) are the three biggest sales categories for Kobo, both in units and money. Science Fiction (all of the science fiction subcategories **combined**) was something like 2.5% of their total sales the last time I checked.

That's my problem, not Kobo's. Small bucket. Lots of other writers. I'm never going to have a lot of sales on Kobo, at least with the current set of rules and assumptions in place. But I know that, and work at the margins to build up my sales, because Kobo is going into places where Amazon either hasn't gone yet, or flamed out for one reason or another. Those are fans I have yet to reach, who might want to buy my books.

Remember, I have lots of books. If I get one fan, that person can spend a nice chunk of money just walking my Kobo catalog. And they'll tell their friends. I'll get there, but it will take me longer.

Series Pages

Getting back to Amazon (and Kobo), though, we need to talk about series pages. Since you are writing several novels in a row about the same characters, those are a series. Both Amazon and Kobo will set up a Series Page for you. In order to create a series page, you generally have to poke Amazon. However, at this time, they're pretty good about automatically adding new books to the series page. Here's a link to the help page. Follow the instructions there: https://kdp.amazon.com/en_US/help/topic/G201757800

They understand that series sell, so they are working to increase their own income, and tend to be pretty friendly folks about it.

As an example, here's a link to the series page on Amazon for Jessica: My Book

The thing about the series page is that now you can advertise the series as a thing, where you were working to sell Book One before, in order to draw the reader in. They want series. Long and rich and deep and interesting. Having a series page means that they'll take a good look at you. May even just HAVE to give you money, which is the fundamental goal here. Plus, the Amazon series page has a "**Buy all the books**" button. This makes it easy for readers to glut themselves on all the books, which is what we want.

And check on the series page every time you add a new book. It usually takes a little while (week or two so you might have to poke them), but that's a factor of the million new books being published this year. And next. And the year after.

You'll want to factor Series Pages into your marketing, and we'll come back to it, but it is a powerful tool you get for just a little work.

Goodreads

So there is a website now owned (I believe) by Amazon, called Goodreads. Readers can sign up and rate books they have read. They can find other books by the same author, or related ones. They can geek out with other readers. They have fun.

The UI is a complete pain in the ass for an author to use. I often wonder if they do that deliberately, because the few times I have wanted to upload my own books to the Goodreads site and claim them, I have had to ask their customer support folks to intervene. And I used to design websites for a living, so I know how easy it can be done.

My advice is to just set yourself up, and claim your titles if you can. From there, ignore the site, except to answer any fan questions that come along, as fast as you can. I log in maybe annually at this point, because I have found the experience so painful. If you can make it work for you, that's another avenue to send your blogs, and interact with folks from a social media standpoint, but I don't think Goodreads actually wants you as a person, so much as a brand others can talk about when you aren't there.

But don't ignore their actual existence.

Reviews

Eventually, you'll get reviews of your books. Another dirty secret I have heard rumors of is that Amazon doesn't count the average rating of the book when deciding who to market, but just the raw number of reviews. I have no way to tell, but I suspect that Amazon understands the basic facets of human personalities on the interwebs. Especially those that bother to leave reviews.

Some people are just assholes. Don't take it personally.

I have a pricing structure. Short stories are $0.99. Novellas run $2.99. Novels go up from $3.99 depending on the length. Anybody looking at my catalog can see that.

Got a one star review that went like this: "Loved the book, but I feel cheated because it's just a short story and he charged me ninety-nine cents for it. It should be free. Other writers sell me whole novels for that price."

The best part for me were all the other fans leaving reviews who utterly savaged that dude, because it says right at the top how long it is and the blurb said short story.

Not everyone will like your book. Fewer will leave you reviews. Only the people at the two ends (loved it, hated it) will generally leave you reviews anyway.

Don't ever read your own reviews, except where someone left you five stars. It is just better for your sanity and your *wa* to have someone else read them for you.

But you do need to count them at least, and fairly often (monthly, maybe).

Recently, I screwed up a pre-order. Right cover. Right blurb. Wrong interior. Started getting emails from fans and bad reviews (by the next morning, mind you, when they had stayed up all night to read the whole novel, knowing it was the wrong novel) that they loved the story, but I had screwed up.

Got it fixed pretty quickly. Sent people bookfunnel links (do you know about Book Funnel?) so they could download the right story, while we worked with Amazon to get the fix in place and notify everyone that they could pull the right file down now.

Important to pay attention to these things. Don't take the reviews personally. And work to get more of them.

Now, on to something I call Physical Media.

Physical Media (and other things)

Business Cards: Business

I was originally going to talk about just print books here, but this is a marketing theme, so there are a couple of other things I want to cover first, before we get to the books themselves. (And, let's face it, print books are a rounding error on my income, not the primary source right now. Working on it, but…)

The first thing you need as a *PROFESSIONAL* (artist, writer, musician, whatever you are) are business cards. Subtle, well-executed, up-to-date. When you meet someone who wants to remain in contact, you need to be able to immediately pull out a business card that has all your contact information on it and hand it to her. No fumbling. No looking for a pen to fix anything. Just pull the card and hand it over like a pro.

It doesn't have to have much on it. Mine say "Blaze Ward. Storyteller" at the top, with my email address and Knotted Road Press's url (my publisher) at the bottom. That's it. No phone number, because I rarely answer my phone unless you are already programmed in. Nothing cute. If you write one genre only, and have an exceptional tagline for it, you might consider, but I write in several, so Storyteller is sufficient. And explanatory.

This is for when you make a professional contact with

someone. Another artist. A prospective publisher or editor. Someone you want to maintain a professional relationship with, so you need to look impressive.

Going back to my author friend who has a very memorable email address that is impossible to spell, this is when you need something simple and easy to use. Since you already own your own domain (RIGHT?) and have set up an email account for you the brand that's exactly the email you want here. Use your gmail or Hotmail as a burner.

If you still have a yahoo or AOL email that you expect to be your professional portal, be prepared to be mocked by some and treated as Junior Varsity by others. Even gmail says to me that you haven't stepped up to act like a pro.

You@yourwebsite.com should be how people interact with you. Everything is about driving traffic to the one place you will be able to control forever, so why cut corners here?

Also, because someone just pointed this out to me, get standard-sized business cards. Two inches tall by three and a half wide. Paper stock. Rectangular. I had someone once hand me her card. It was one inch tall and three inches wide, so it didn't fit into any of the places in my wallet where I would store it and I had to stuff it in a pocket. I lost it pretty quickly. Lost her contact information. Got it eventually, like a year later when I saw her at a con, but that was a year later.

I don't care how cute you think they are. You want to be seen here as a serious professional, not a flouncy *artisté*. This is the time to act like one. They're really cheap and you can order them by the 500 load when you get to that part. Carry them everywhere you go, and expect to be able to hand them to someone and be good.

Business Cards: Marketing

The other kind of business card I carry is the marketing card. Still 3.5" x 2" as is standard in North America and easy to store and carry. On the front is one of my covers. (Usually *Auberon*, since that's Book One of a long series.). It is slightly cropped to fit the format, but has the exact cover, with title, image, and author on it.

You want to be able to have the person holding the card open up Amazon or Kobo and immediately recognize that they have the right book.

On the back: Title across the top. Series name right below that. The actual blurb for the book below that, and then a quick note from the publisher at the bottom, with my url (www.blazeward.com) clear at the last.

Why: "Oh, you're a writer? What do you write?"

Bang, out comes the *Auberon* card. Or *Science Officer*. Or whatever. I immediately hand it to them. They hold it. The cover is awesome. They flip it over and read the blurb. If they like SF, they probably will like Jessica Keller.

They keep the card, even when they try to hand it back. I buy these by the 500-load for $10, give or take. Hell, I'll leave them tacked to bulletin boards and randomly abandoned on tables at coffee ships. Cheap. If I sell three copies of the novel, I've broken even on the box. Walked into a restaurant for lunch today and the waitress remembered me from several weeks earlier, and apologized that her TBR pile was still too big, but she was planning to get my book. She had the card. Had touched it. Knew it and knew who I was. (How awesome is that?)

Why is this important? Psychology tells us, after a lot of studies on advertising, that you need to put the name of your product in front of someone roughly four times before it sinks in.

One: They read the card and keep it, putting it someplace *safe*, like a wallet or purse.

Two: They forget about the card until they get home, and pull it out of a pocket, or find it in the wallet a week or three later. The card gets put on a dresser or bookshelf to remember.

Three: A week passes and they keep looking at the card without really seeing it.

Four: Something finally clicks and they go look up the series. And the fact that I have a LOT of books they could read, if they wanted to read.

Business cards. Nothing smaller. Absolutely nothing larger. I lose custom bookmarks so fast I'm convinced that fairies come at night and steal them for some esoteric purpose. (One of my First Readers came back later and admitted he was paneling his den with all the bookmarks he had stolen from me.) Anything smaller gets lost. Some people do postcards, but 4" x 6" is way too big to even stuff in a pocket and not lose.

You want to insert yourself into their mind the easiest way you can. Science is on your side with the business card, at least in modern, North American culture. Make it work for you.

Business Cards: BookFunnel

Bookfunnnel (http://www.bookfunnel.com/) is a service the publisher pays for. You put your ebook files up and Damon (the amazing and awesome Damon, especially when singing and dancing) sends you a link. You can sell the link to people, from your own website (an intermediate task we'll cover in a later book), or you can get labels from the office supply store and print these links to be stuck onto the back of your marketing cards.

They can be single-use, meaning that it only works once. They can be set to a fixed number of downloads. Or they can be limited by a deadline date. Your choice. Very convenient to use. Very easy for a random reader to understand.

If you are going to an event, you can print some bookfunnel codes on labels and stick them to the back of your marketing business cards, and give people a free book. (Great for Book One in a long series you want to hook them on.) I've done this. We've also sold ebooks for ninety-nine cents at others. Hand them a card already printed out and go.

You can even just give them out for free to random strangers, if the book is already only $0.99US and you want them engaged. I have done this more than once.

Low cost, high return. Puts all the information you need them to have IN THEIR HANDS. Gives them a prize for acting quickly. Sets the hook.

THE KEY in all of these circumstances is that Americans (and many other Westerners) are prepared to deal with business cards. They won't have to remember your name or the name of your book when they get home several hours later. They can hand the card off to their cousin who is totally into that sort of thing.

The information gets transmitted without error. The fan can find you again later. The pro you are talking to can send an email about a job they know that you might be perfect for. The damned things are cheap.

Take advantage of it.

Also, for you mid-functioning introverts, you don't EVER have to explain your book. Hand them the card and hide behind it while they read and absorb. Minimal human interaction, but still the possibility of a sale. Win/Win.

Print Books

Okay, so now on to paper books. This marketing volume came about because of a conversation I was having with a friend who lives near Atlanta, Georgia. He is one of the hardest working hustlers I know, forever trying to get the local, independent book stores in the region to carry his various books. Doing cons and signings. Never stopping in a decade of busting his ass (so far). Man impresses the hell out me every day when he talks about what he's doing next.

His logic (at least as I understand it, so blame me for mistakes, and not him) is that you have already filtered for readers, by having your book(s) in a book store. You have filtered for people looking for more than just the latest TradPub bestseller by being in a small, local store. Many buyers want to support local businesses, which is why they are in a small bookstore in the first place. Adding "Local Author" on the cover or the shelf ought to trigger something in the buyer that they'll at least pick up the book and study it.

MORE PUBLISHER RULES: *There are other books out there that can help you with the right cover, the right blurb, and the right "heft" for lack of a better term to describe that new book feel and smell. Go read them and make sure your books are at least as professional looking as what New York puts out.*

I can't stress enough that you need to be indistinguishable from TradPub, in terms of the actual thing they hold in their hands or see on their reader screen. A decade ago, any cover was probably good enough, because there was so little product and people were ravenous. Now you need to look like a pro. That includes pretty interiors, so I am going to take a moment to suggest one of the new tools of the latest revolution in Indie. It is worth your time, if you are going to write a lot.

Vellum (https://vellum.pub/) is a program you can currently only buy for the Mac. It allows me to format a Microsoft Word *.docx file and a cover image into a pretty book in about 15 minutes. Read that again. 15 minutes. How many hours did you spend doing your most recent book in whatever older tools you have been using? How much time were you *NOT WRITING*?

If you plan to publish two books this year, Vellum is not a useful investment. My wife and I plan to publish at least thirty novels. And more next year. I can format my own books, and that includes epub, mobi, pdf (print), and apple formatting. In about 15 minutes. (If you're really only doing a couple of books a year, use the Draft2Digital templates for creating your ebooks. You'll currently still have to pay someone to create your interiors for print books, but D2D has a beta program for automatically doing that already in place that will hopefully be rolled out sometime in 2019. That will start the next revolution, most likely.)

The reason I bring this up is that Vellum puts out pretty

interiors. You want pretty interiors. Readers know what they subconsciously expect a book's interior to be like, based on a century of TradPub. You need your interior to look polished and pretty, so readers don't put it down, right at the moment when they've liked your cover, approved of the blurb, and flipped it open to read the first few pages.

But...

If you are relying on print books in bookstores for your sales, you won't ever get there. Especially not as an Indie. According to some rumors I have heard but not verified closely, something like 75% of print sales now occur on-line, rather than in bookstores, so people are ordering their next book from B&N.com or Amazon, rather than walking into the corner bookstore to buy it.

Additionally you generally just won't make as much on a printed book as you do an ebook, regardless of where someone buys it. The math is brutal, but simple. My apologies, because this is probably going to offend some of you. ("Would you rather be famous or rich?")

How much money would you need to be making annually from your writing to safely walk away from having any day job? (Or retiring the spouse who has been supporting you for all these years?) If you put your print book up on the big print players in extended distribution at the right price point, you should expect to earn back about $2.00USD per book.

Two dollars.

And remember, that $2 comes after you've already had to price your print on demand book higher than a regular paperback. You'll never be able to match mass market paperback prices and turn even $0.02 profit.

How many print books do you need to sell to hit that number you gave me earlier? A whole bunch more than you thought, wasn't it? How many bookstores are in your area? How many of them would you need to hit, and be selling at least one copy every day (which is an astounding number for one title or even one author, if you ask a bookstore owner), to make enough every month to be secure?

A whole freaking bunch.

Back when you could be on the shelf at every major book chain in the country, it might have worked. Borders and Waldenbooks are both gone and B&N carries pretty much just the best-sellers and a few other things. You aren't even really mid-list yet, and there is almost no mid-list left for you to join.

So why bother with print books?

Because there are readers out there who like something physical on their shelves. I get to sign books every once in a while because somewhere I picked up fans. (Yeah, I don't know either.) Look up and tell me how many books you can see from where you're sitting right now. You are probably just as bad as me. Bunches.

Plus, you can take them to conventions and shows and stuff and maybe have a table where your pretty books are sitting there for folks to wander by and fall in love with. A book purchased, according to the numbers from an expert I trust, should eventually go through something like six hands, meaning a lot of people will have a chance to read it and decide to buy your catalog. (That's going to take years or perhaps decades, but it might happen.)

However, most readers today would rather read books on their magic tablet. Or their phone. Those are ebooks. Take me for example. I have a library card, and can download ebooks to read.

So let's circle back to Kobo, the Canadian company owned by Rakuten, that is going head to head with Amazon in the ebook space. They are aggressively partnering with whoever the local bookstore chain is in the country they want to target next, to provide that dominant player a huge catalog of books they can sell with a small amount of infrastructure. Again, ebooks.

More interestingly, however, is that group of readers called "the next billion." These are generally people and countries coming up from relative poverty and working towards the middle class of whatever place they live. Whole countries are developing this way.

Wanna know how those people will acquire and read books? On their phone. Wireless delivery, once micropayments and sophisticated banking is in place. No need to store heavy, paper books. Able to read anywhere. Perhaps a billion new folks joining us as readers. E-readers.

The physical media book world is mature and generally saturated. All of TradPub has been reporting declining sales of paper books for a decade now. I especially love the part every year where they proclaim that the era of the ebook is over and that paper sales are poised for a comeback.

Their losses might be flattening out, but the truth is that TradPub represents a smaller and smaller portion of total book sales (print and ebook) every year. Indies like you and I are eating their lunch, by publishing off-the-grid, as it were. Those big conglomerates are frequently relying on a couple dozen "trusted" bookstores to report sales, and extrapolating outward from that. Better, I saw a newspaper article recently, by a major player, talking about how the median income for writers had actually gone down.

Gosh, they got nearly 5,000 responses to their annual survey? I'm guessing that there are significantly more than 50,000 writers out there that they didn't hear from, just in the US. And then they used "lies, damned lies, and statistics" to make their case, by using the median. Dirty little secret? If the pool of writers keeps growing, the median generally has to go down, because that is the mid-point where half of all incomes reported are above, and half below. If you made $1,000 this year, for example as you started, you pull those numbers down, even as you started your climb up to a successful career. You and a lot of friends.

Okay, so I have vented about a number of interlocking issues that seem to tie up too many young writers into the wrong mindset (IMO) and damage their careers in bad ways, mostly because TradPub (et al) has no clue about how to make money in the future.

Print books are lovely, and useful as a marketing tool, but they won't make you rich. Getting the local bookstore to carry them won't get you out of a dayjob. Going to cons and having a table to sell your books at won't do it either. (Hell, I'm not sure you do more than break even, once all expenses are factored in, if you have to travel at all.)

Time = Money.

The time you are spent on these hustles is admirable, and my hat is off to you for doing it, but I want you to sit down now and take a hard look at the actual income that you earned from them over the last year. And do it with your publisher hat on, not the writer hat that is excited to be able to walk into a bookstore and see your name on the shelf. I get that same jolt of excitement that you do. Doesn't pay my bills.

Okay, so you got the numbers in your head, or at your fingertips?

Would you have been better off spending more of that time writing? At the speed I write, that probably represents a couple of novels worth of effort. As I mentioned earlier, in my opinion (and others who taught me), the best marketing you can do for your career is to write the next book.

Why?

Critical Mass

It used to be (TradPub days, so before maybe 1980, give or take) that your publisher worked with you over several early novels to hone your craft, find your voice, and build your audience. That doesn't happen anymore.

The rumors and stories I hear from folks better in tune with that sort of thing is that your book has to make a certain sales number on Week One. It comes out on a Tuesday. By the end of the next Monday, TradPub has already decided if they are going to give you a contract for your second book. Brutal. Efficient for them, but brutal. If you just published the first book of a trilogy, there might never be Two and Three. Your career, as far as TradPub is concerned, is over. (Oh, and you can't even ask for the rights to that book back for 35 years. Put a reminder in your calendar.)

Worse, in those archaic days the rule of thumb was something along the lines that you needed to have something like 8-12 novels in print in order to be making a comfortable living from your residuals alone. No more day job. And that's was a nice, middle-class living in those old days, not scraping by in a dump and eating cat food.

The Indie Revolution upended that. They did it by publishing something on the order of one million new books each year for the last several years. 1,000,000 ballpark. That's a lot of product, and proof that the gatekeepers in New York were suppressing things. Not all of the stuff coming out today is good. Some of it is utter crap, but crap sinks quickly, and every book has a few fans, no matter how bad.

With the rise of series logic, now fans want more. They might not buy your series until they know it is done, or far enough along that you'll finish it. (Thanks, GRRM.)

More recently, the logic has changed. The last few years, it looked like you needed to have maybe *twenty* novels out, and in some tight series and extended universes, in order to be making good money. That's part of the reason I talked about the story/novel/series/EU earlier. That's where things seem to be going right now, and what you'll need to face up to as you build your career.

RULES REMINDER: *You are responsible for your own career.*

As more people put out more product, those numbers are going to probably keep going up. You'll need to have twenty-five novels in a single genre soon. And then maybe thirty, in order to be making enough money, because you are competing with every other writer out there for mindshare, and all the other places people can spend their entertainment dollars. Videos. Games. Etc.

One of the current marketing trends (2019) is called "Twenty Books To 50k" and that's their logic. Twenty novels should get you to a $50,000USD/annum income. Probably even works for a few more years.

I expect the next revolution in Indie (ETA roughly mid 2020-2021) to upend things yet again, so I don't know what that future is like. Don't care either. This book is for basic marketing things you need to be doing so you are prepared to face that future. The Intermediate book I want to do soon will try to address some of those things, because they'll be the things I think will work tomorrow, and maybe not the day after.

Print Book Pricing

So I've talked pros and cons on print books. You are responsible for your own career, so take my advice with a pinch (or lick) of salt. But understand why I say what I do, and don't just automatically discount it because someone else told you different. Are they making as much money as I am from their writing? If so, listen to them (and tell me what you learn, so I can start doing it and incorporate it into a future book for everyone else). If they aren't selling that well, question why they think that path will work. It might for them. It might for you. This one is working well for me and I'm trying to help others get farther along. YMMV

You have a print book. It's pretty. The cover nails genre. The blurb is enticing and leave you breathless. Your opening paragraph is perfect.

How do you price it?

Most services will give you a number that is the raw cost to actually print and deliver the book somewhere. On top of that, there is the royalty cost to the author (you in the other hat). Finally, there is the profit. (Warning: more math ahead.)

In extended distribution, the bookstores need to be able to make a profit of at least $2.00 US on any given book before they will even touch it. So round everything up to the nearest $.99 value, maybe more, but always ending in 99 for US markets. (UK and European markets generally prefer 49 as a number.)

Also, you need to take into account that many independent bookstores automatically do a 10% or maybe 20% discount on new books, just as a way to draw in foot traffic.

In the past, I have priced books following the old patterns and not seen much movement in print, even as my ebook sales have continued to climb. However, the world has changed.

In 2018, Amazon made a huge adjustment, moving everything from CreateSpace as the service doing their print books to Kindle Direct Print (KDP). New rules. New everything. And because it was going to be such a massive pain in the ass to set everything up again, almost from scratch, a lot of small publishers like me looked at finally moving everything over to Ingram-Spark as their print distributor.

BUSINESS RULE: *It's okay to make changes to your product, but you should never make such a massive disruption that the customer has to start over. If you do, why should they not take the time to look at your competitors? Never break the lock-in factor and loyalty you have built up over time.*

Amazon shot themselves in the foot with this one. And then rolled out a pretty buggy beta product to replace something that just worked fine. Lots of us fled.

So in 2019, my books will still be available to Amazon shoppers in the store, but now I'm in the much broader marketplace that Ingram-Spark offers. So I need to rethink my print book pricing.

It is useful to note here that an American writer will need to buy ISBN numbers in order to publish on Ingram-Spark, while a print book on Amazon can just have one issued.

Originally, in addition to the expensive print book editions, I also had what we called an ASE, or Amazon Special Edition. Those books were only priced at $9.99. We ended up selling more books at that price point than the higher one, but not that many.

I had a long talk recently with a friend of mine who owns an independent bookstore. Ran over some of my old logic, and then asked him his logic for carrying new books. He tries to offer things at about a 20% discount, so significantly less than cover price, but that meant that the profit margin listed above was largely gone, and they would end up only making pennies on one of my books, rather than dollars, so it was unlikely that he would carry them unless someone ordered it in print from him.

That honesty was one of the reasons I like the guy and trust him with questions like that.

So this year we're going to look instead at putting the print book prices back up at the $14.99 or $19.99 price point, so that bookstores will have a reason to carry my novels. The Amazon Special Editions ($9.99) that worked for my superfans actually seems to work to suppress my print sales from bookstores. My mistake, and one I'm looking at fixing by making them go away. (Or maybe the world just changed from under me and this is one of those regular course corrections people need to do. Everything needs to be reviewed regularly and corrected if you find out you are wrong, like I was.)

The problem here is what is called *Showrooming*. A person walks into a store and finds something they like. They immediately pull out their phone and compare prices on Amazon to what they have in hand. If they can order it and get it that much cheaper, they will. If they break about even, they might want to walk out the door with the widget.

Books can be delivered to your home. Ebooks can go straight to the magic book or phone for reading. You'll need to actually set the prices of your paper books high enough to entice bookstores, and then not allow Amazon to have it at a cheaper price.

Live and learn. Hopefully, I'll actually start moving some

paper if/when we get there, but I'm still making more profit on a $5.99 ebook novel (about $4.00USD), than I am on a $19.99 print book (around $2.00USD), so my emphasis doesn't change.

Print Marketing

I am not telling you to stop the bookstore hustle. I do it some, just not anywhere nearly as aggressively as other writers I know. The trade show/con circuit is also a good way to market books. My cousin Rachel does that all the time and usually sells out of her stack of books before Sunday morning.

But she's an extrovert. The thought of spending all that time talking to random strangers makes my skin crawl. I can do it. Did it rather well at a recent Rose City Comic Con in Portland, OR. But I had to become somebody else for the whole weekend to pull it off, and I got NO WRITING DONE that weekend as a result. F@#$ that noise.

If you are an extrovert, go for it. I'm a high-functioning introvert. I'd rather spend my time writing, because those hours are more likely to make me more profit long term.

Print books are absolutely a marketing tool, because people in a bookstore have money burning a hole in their pocket and you're in front of them. Fans at (the right) con are the same way. (RCCC fans were not generally interested in SF, preferring Urban Fantasy by a wide margin.)

These people want to give you money. People can make the con circuit work.

I don't know many of them that make a living at it. They have a day job and do this on the weekend. They have a bookstore and hit the big cons to make a little extra splash and reach new customers.

My goal (and hopefully yours) is to make a living writing. I don't think this is a profitable use of much time. It might work for you. It has not for me.

But you are responsible for your own career. Find your niche and your hustle, and make them work for you. Just understand that you need to look at the numbers occasionally and be honest with yourself about them.

Outright Bribery

One kinda off-beat topic to talk about, but one that falls loosely into the physical media concept.

When people sign up for my newsletter, one of the things I'm going to start doing is giving away a short story I wrote. Here, download this ebook and enjoy it.

Don't be afraid to give away books to your fans. One sale isn't going to make or break your career, but it might just cement them as a fan, and that's more money and friends later on, when it will be important.

Recently, I had a dude contact me with a very mild complaint about a trilogy of books coming out in 2019 (CS-405), and how they were short and more than he wanted to budget for the print editions. Was I going to do an omnibus edition in print?

Until that moment, I had never even considered it, but it made perfect sense once he asked. However, I wouldn't do an omnibus of the whole trilogy until much later, so as to not cannibalize sales, and this was the CS-405 books, which contained too many details for him to make sense of the 8th Jessica Keller novel without reading.

Rather than make him wait a whole year to finish the series, by holding off for the omnibus, I just sent him the three titles in ebook format, with a promise from him that he'll eventually buy the omnibus when it comes out. Couple of bucks for me was less important than making sure I had a happy fan here. And ebooks do not cost anything to you, once they are generated.

Don't be afraid to give them to fans. Or bribe folks with them.

Social Media

The Platforms

So we've already talked about the need for you to have your own website. To own the url. To have an email system in place. To make it look simple, clean, and professional. Some of you are already bitching at me because you've got a social media presence elsewhere and why do you need to have something that's expensive to acquire and maintain?

Angelfire.

AOL. LiveJournal. Six Degrees. Friendster. Are you seeing a trend here? They're all gone. Anything you had on them in the way of friends, messages, or pictures? Gone. MySpace is still there. When was the last time you logged into your account?

Churn and change is the nature of the business. There will always be a need for some sort of social media tool online, to allow distant groups of folks (friends, fans, former coworkers) to stay in touch with one another. As I write these words, Facebook is the largest player, utterly dominant right now in ways that nobody else ever really managed until they did.

And they appear to have inflected. Fewer actual users. (I saw an article in Jan 2019 suggesting that as much as 50% of their reported user base were actually fake accounts. Trolls. Hackers.

Whatever.) They are seeing people move away from the platform, and those remaining are spending less time on it.

You can have a lovely author page set up, with special groups for your fans and curation that makes it a wonderful experience. But the generation coming up (Kids, these days. Heh) aren't using their grandparent's tools. (I suspect that they will eventually, just so they can stay in touch with grandma, but…). They are using other tools that aren't as large, aren't as generic, and won't have as big a user base.

I'm not even going to bother trying to list them, because that list will be out of date before this books hits print. What you need to do is go ask your tween or teen what platforms they use to stay in touch with their friends.

Because the big, current players worked so hard to monetize things, the next generation are going elsewhere. (If you aren't paying for the product, bubba, then you ARE the product.) Because the big players maintain extensive data warehouses of everything someone posted or liked, the kids are moving to companies that let them encrypt messages, and (supposedly) don't keep copies of those messages.

It is a lovely idea, and I'm proud of the kids for recognizing early that their data has value, and you either need to pay them for it, or they won't share.

But. (Yup, there's that word again.)

If your small social media platform cannot monetize users somehow, they will go out of business. Everyone is willing to throw money at founders, looking for THE NEXT BIG THING, but at some point, the money runs out. On that day, you better be turning a profit, or finding a way to sell your company to one of the big girls.

Tumblr used to be the sort of free-for-all that let people link up with others like them, without the fear of the morality police cracking down hard on them. But they couldn't make money fast enough, so they eventually ended up being bought by Verizon, the American telephone company. In Dec 2018, new rules came into place limiting the sorts of things the corporate overlords allowed on the site.

Dunno if they were successful in retaining any sort of user base after that, because my response to the new rules was to simply delete my account and walk away. And never look back, because there will be someone else eventually. There always is.

So if you had a major Tumblr presence, are all your fans gone now? Multiply that by every other social media company out there and you'll begin to understand the risks to your career inherent in letting someone else set the rules.

At the same time, you should be cognizant that that's where you can find and interact with fans. But there are too many platforms to be on, and they all do something different. You could spend all your time maintaining a dozen online accounts in various places.

How much would you get done? Keep that in mind. We'll circle back to it in the next chapter.

Pick one, and only one, if you are up to the concept of "doing social media" and stick with it. They all do different things, so they have different rules for how you need to operate. Some are interactive (Facebook is a good example), while others are much more one-way (Pinterest and Instagram, among the big players). Some are strictly a communications platform between two people. While that's a great way to interact with a fan, that's ONE fan, when you need to be building yourself to hundreds and maybe thousands eventually.

Whatever you do, make sure you have a big enough megaphone that you can reach the most people for the LEAST AMOUNT OF WORK ON YOUR PART. That's the key. Do it, but WIBBOW on everything. More novels generally equals more money. Lots of fan interaction that keeps you from writing eventually kills your career. (Think GRRM and GoT.)

Social media can be helpful, but understand that every platform has a life cycle. It's born. People discover it. It becomes the next big thing. People become bored or offended. They have a Yogi Berra moment ("Nobody ever goes there because it's always so crowded."). They go find something that is more personal to offset the old platform.

Angelfire. AOL. LiveJournal. Six Degrees. Friendster. Myspace. Facebook.

What will you have when the next one shuts down? Or when all your fans migrate to twenty different places all at once, so you can't affordably chase them?

You'll have **you.com** with everything they need in order to stay up to date.

The near future is a narrowcasting one, where one platform can't reach everyone, and you'll need to think defensively as a result.

Marketing Is Not Social Media

I'm gonna come back and harp on this a little more, because I've gotten into more than one social altercation with folks who would read the section above and tell me I don't know a damned thing. Maybe. How many books did you sell last year?

Your marketing efforts need to exist on one or more social media platforms, but those efforts need to be independent of any of them. You don't want your career tied to the success of Myspace. Or Friendster. Or any of the rest of them.

You will market on social media platforms. Goodreads is a passive thing that appears to be better off set up once and then left to your fans and their system to manage. Believe me, I've tried to keep it up to date and when I gave up trying they still have a shitty interface that required me to pretty much send someone on their helpdesk an email to get things corrected, as I mentioned earlier.

WIBBOW

And while we're at it, at what point does social media pass the WIBBOW test? I realize that YMMV, but you need to be writing first and marketing second. The whole of the passive nature of this is that one blog can touch fans everywhere, without you having to spend a great deal of time on any of them.

Amazon is also a social media platform, and one more especially dedicated to readers. If you go look at your Amazon Author page, you'll see all your recent blog posts across the page. (If yours isn't already set up, here's a link to mine for comparison. https://www.amazon.com/Blaze-Ward/e/B00K3X2VFQ/). And go look on the left, where the [+ Follow] button is and you'll see the "About Blaze Ward" right below that, and then the "Sign up for Blaze's VIP newsletter…" right below that.

My point here is that you need to centralize yourself so that you can set up passive accounts in other places and push out your blog and newsletter and such and let fans find you, rather than spending all your time trying to chase them. My blog goes to FB, Amazon, Goodreads, and others. I don't care how you found me. I want you to be able to see all my books and decide that you need to read more of them.

Additional Note: An early reader asked for more detail about how to set up your blog to automatically feed to places like Amazon, Goodreads, Facebook, and the rest. I'm using Wordpress for my website. It has a plug in that allows me to post directly to Facebook as a push. For the others, you will need to set up your account there, and then configure it with an rss feed from your website in order to do a pull. Wordpress makes this easy for you by automatically generating an rss feed url that you can just copy and paste.

If all of that was Greek, there are folks you can ask who will generally be willing to help if you buy them beer or pizza.

Marketing Decisions

MARKETING VERSUS ADVERTISING

So what is the difference between these two terms: Marketing and Advertising? I'm going to go ahead and quote a website that goes into better detail than I can if you want to deep-dive on the topic. (https://www.thebalancesmb.com/marketing-vs-advertising-what-s-the-difference-2294825)
Remember, that we're at a beginner level here, just setting a baseline up so we can move on later to intermediate things. (I plan to write a B4B: Marketing for the Intermediate Publisher later, after I figure out how well some of my current plans have worked. Stay tuned.)

"***Marketing*** *is the systematic planning, implementation, and control of a mix of activities intended to bring together buyers and sellers for the mutually advantageous exchange or transfer of products or services.*"

"***Advertising*** *is only one component of the overall* ***marketing*** *process. Advertising is that part of marketing that involves directly getting the word out about your business, product, or service to those you want to reach most.*"

In this book, I'm going to generally refer to advertising as the act of setting up a formal campaign, such as ads on Facebook or Amazon, in order to let readers know that there is something new for them to know about and discover. Marketing is the overall (larger) process whereby you set yourself up to look indistinguishable from a major publisher as a stone professional, and all the little things you can do along the way to make sure that once someone has heard you, they can find you and your books and buy them all.

Passive Marketing versus Active

Passive herein means that you set it up once, and then pretty much leave it alone, except to occasionally update and review things. A good example is your landing page on you.com, where you list the most recent two or three books, and what's coming out soon. Fix that only as frequently as you put things up for pre-order. Monthly, perhaps.

Active is where you are doing things that require a lot of your personal time (or the expense of your Virtual Assistant or loving spouse to do things). Running targeted ad campaigns on bookbub, with a lot of A/B testing and a high spend rate, where you have to check the numbers constantly for several hours, is active marketing. There are books you can read and classes you can take that will teach you how to actively and aggressively market your books. And they will work, at least in the short term.

However, I have seen many people who spend a lot of time doing the active marketing thing, and they end up being quite successful at it. Eventually, though, they forget to write books and end up just pimping the same six novels for several years. They are forever up on a treadmill of having to find more readers, because the ones they had have read everything and now moved on.

That, to me, is always the central tenet, the central failure of active marketing. WIBBOW. I'm a writer, not a marketer, so I want to write. I won't be as successful as you over the short term.

I will have a much longer career than you do. But that's your career. Do what works best for you.

Freebies and Perma-free

There is an entire sub-genre of readers who only want free books. Romance has done itself badly by aggressively going as close to zero as possible, to the point that many Romance writers have to price at a much lower point than I do with my Science Fiction. Not all of them, but lots and lots.

Pricing becomes a genre-specific thing that you need to understand. (This is exactly why I harped on you to understand your genre and shelf decisions earlier.) Romance is largely a bargain genre, where your books frequently will be free or $0.99USD in order to drive traffic. Mystery, at the other end of the price spectrum, is usually a high-price genre, partly because mystery readers consider themselves the smartest folks out there. If they see a mystery for really cheap, they just assume that it is crap and won't buy it. Dunno. YMMV.

Science fiction sits in the middle. I can charge a nice price for my books ($3.99 - $6.99 depending on length), make a nice margin (Amazon and others are at around 68% of cover net), and make a nice living.

RULE: *What genre your writer works in determines what you can do to price things. Usually.*

Once you have a series going, a common, relatively-passive technique, is to drop the price of Book One to either cheap ($0.99US for me) or free. Amazon won't actually let you do free directly, because they want their share of the money, but if you drop the price to free on Kobo, Amazon will quickly match it on their site and stay there as long as you do.

Both *The Science Officer* and *Auberon* are generally at $0.99US, because they are each the first book in respectively long series. At that price folks are willing to take a flyer and by it. And both are good enough stories on their own that I can hook most readers. (My read-through for the *Science Officer* series, from volumes 1 through 8, is generally about 60%, meaning that more than half the people who read #1 bought #8.)

When you have enough novels in a series, one of the other passive marketing things you can try is to drop book one permanently to free or ninety-nine cents, and then set book two at $2.99 (the magic price on Amazon and others where they start to pay you the best royalty). Starting with books three through the end is where you make your profit.

However, understand that this really only works for you when you have five or more novels in a single series. And a friend of mine just dropped book fourteen in his latest series (#14!!!). He has a long tail upon which he can make up for all the people that bought the first few at cheap prices.

The problem with permafree, in my opinion and conversations with some readers, is that you get two kinds of readers. The first won't read anything but free books, so they snag it because it is free, but then go on to whoever else had a free book they could download next. Very few of those people convert into paying customers.

The other kind are casual fans of your genre who came across it and figured that it sounded good enough to download. Their problem is that they don't have anything invested in actually going and reading your book until they finish up with all their favorites, many of whom might be flooding the market with product. By the time they get around to you, they might have forgotten why they downloaded it and never get around to actually reading it.

At $0.99, they have had to pay something for my book, so they want to see what they are getting for it. Different mindset.

Now, one thing I have tried is the short-term freebie. Kobo lets you try to sign up for all sorts of interesting promotions. Recently, I dropped *Auberon* to free on Kobo as part of a deal, but only for a single week, right after Christmas. Amazon matched it within hours. In that week, 206 free downloads of *Auberon* on Kobo. By the end of January (when I'm writing this), I have eight sales of book two, *Queen Of The Pirates*, up from the usual none or extremely few. *Last Of The Immortals* and *Goddess of War* both have six sales each, and later books in the series are at about four, but that's probably just people reading at different paces.

My (admittedly rounding-error level) sales on Kobo are about double in January from what they were in December, and maybe two and a half times the previous level. We'll see if that holds. I seem to have picked up eight new fans, mostly in Canada, but apparently one in Singapore. (Yeah, I don't know either, but I'm not complaining. Hopefully, she'll tell a friend about me.)

Them nickels spend, too.

Over on Amazon, that same freebie period generated 879 downloads for Auberon over the first week of the year. For the rest of the month so far, I've moved about a quarter that many copies of *Auberon* at $0.99. And I've still moved more copies of *Auberon* at the higher price this month than I have *Queen Of The Pirates*.

Maybe I was successful. Maybe not. I can see six prospective new fans on Kobo. I can assume a few dozen new ones on Amazon. This was successful for me because I spent about 15 minutes total setting it up and getting the approval of the wonderful ladies at Kobo who curate these things. I'm hoping to hook each of those people into $100USD or so, once they walk my catalog. Then nickels spend.

But this was a special deal on Kobo. A "ONE WEEK ONLY! HURRY!!!" kind of thing that plays on human psychology to get that damned book for free while they can. And I got maybe twenty-five new fans, out of just about eleven hundred downloads. The math sucks, but the costs to me were sufficient that I'll do it again.

What I've seen of perma-free is that even that 25/1100 conversion rate might be kinda high. If they aren't paying for it, they aren't emotionally engaged in it.

Understanding Advertising

So there are a lot of books out there that purport to teach you how to write good novels. Others will make your blurb spiffy. I have found that one of the best things for me was to read **Joseph Sugarman**'s classic tome: *The Adweek Copywriting Handbook: The Ultimate Guide to Writing Powerful Advertising and Marketing Copy from One of America's Top Copywriters*. And get the paper edition, so you can highlighter the hell out of it like I did.

It is a very old book by our standards, and he has lessons on how he did successful ad campaigns for Citizen Band Radios in magazines in the early 1970's. But once you read it, you will understand that there are certain basics to the field of advertising and human psychology that will not change over time.

And change over time is one of the key lessons I want to impart to you here. At any given moment, there is a particular set of things that work, when you move into active (and sometime aggressive) marketing and advertising techniques. I'm not going to touch them here because by the time you read this book, they may no longer be relevant at all.

That's because everyone who latches onto some facet or technique that seems to work immediately writes a book and starts teaching classes to everyone on how to replicate it as a way to make a shit-ton of money in a short period of time.

Since it usually takes advantage of some quirk in someone else's system, at some point that other person (Amazon, for instance) will tweak something and suddenly whatever it was doesn't work anymore. And Amazon spends a lot of time and energy rebalancing things to give the most writers and the most consumers the best results for their money. (I have a friend who works at Amazon who is only allowed to nod knowingly when I mention that topic. Occasionally with a feral smile when someone has just gotten what they had coming.)

Don't rely on gimmicks. They will fail eventually. Rely on your career, adding more books to your back catalog so your old fans have new things to buy and new fans have a smorgasbord of excitement ahead of them. That has been the best advice anyone has given me to date, and the best thing I think I can tell you.

Given what I have seen and learned over the years, every new trick that comes along has between two and maybe five years at most before they fail. Today's one-perfect-trick won't work next year. That thing you can do that guarantees your that your ads get best placement on an Amazon page fails when everybody else is trying to do it as well, and starts outbidding you for results. Poof.

One of the folks at the top of the advertising game right now gave a talk last fall where he spelled out how many hours he spent every day on his advertising work. It was scary. The A/B tests. The spikes. The bidding strategies he had to adjust on the fly (24/7) so he didn't accidentally spent $5,000US on a campaign. (Yeah, five thousand. He was talking about spending five hundred dollars per day some days, and making it all back, but...)

He was averaging something like five hours per day, just keeping track of the ad campaigns he was running on bookbub. And spending more than most of us make in a day, several days per week.

And you know what? He had largely stopped writing. His latest book on the latest advertising gimmick was already six months late, and he accidentally mentioned that it might not work by the time he got it done. He was so busy going to conventions and events to actually do any writing along the way.

And the man's an extrovert, so he enjoys doing that sort of stuff. That already makes him the two percent among us, and not the ninety-eight percent of introverts. It works for him, but I don't see it working for more than a couple more years at most. After that, he'll have to find a new loophole to exploit.

Another person, a guy who can teach you an amazing amount of information about running ads everywhere, was giving a talk that a friend of mine was at. At some point, he supposedly mentioned off-hand that he was going to be in trouble soon because he had just about run out of ideas for how to keep marketing his half dozen books. Apparently, he spent the rest of the talk doing a lot of hand-waving and jedi mind tricks to try to make people forget that little point that he only had six books for sale.

You can do advertising, and I'll have some ideas below. Don't let it transform you from a writer to a marketer. In both of the cases above, they had stopped writing, so now they had to face running out of fans. At that point, you have to work twice as hard because every sale is now a complete stranger coming along, rather than an old friend coming over for dinner.

This is why I bang repeatedly on this adage.

RULE: *The best advertising you can do is to write your next book.*

Fans will come back and buy it. If you drop something every month, eventually they're going to add a note in their calendar to make sure they came over and bought it. But if you stop writing, and have eight novels to your name, what happens when they have read all eight?

Where do they go?

Writing To Market

I have to touch on this topic, because this is a form of active marketing. And it can be successful, over a very short term, but it won't make you a career.

To write to market is to look at what's selling hot right now, and go write a pastiche in that genre, even though that's not where your heart is. JK Rowling functionally reinvented YA Urban Fantasy with Harry Potter. And did it better than anyone else. Does it. She's that good. But everyone suddenly was writing

Harry Potter knockoffs. Some of them were even pretty good, but a lot of them weren't.

In the gold rush era of a new genre, readers aren't as picky. Actually, they are, but you engage a new kind of reader, so I need to talk about the three flavors of readers now.

Voracious readers eat books. They are the ones who walk out of a used bookstore with two bags full, every week. They read 2-3 books per day. Crazy. They'll try damned near anything, just because they read and need a firehose to keep them full.

Casual readers are the ones who read perhaps a dozen to a score of books per year. Every month or so, give or take. They'll have a genre they like, and a few authors on their list, and will work their way through both. They keep us in business.

Social readers are the ones that only read the latest cultural phenomenon. They are the ones that make TradPub its money, purely on the scale of how many people will rush out to buy that one books, and no others.

There are not that many voracious readers out there. Casual readers keep the bookstores in business, more or less, because they are a large enough contingent that those few buys are multiplied by a deep pool. Social readers picked up Harry Potter because everyone was talking about it. *Hunger Games* was the same way. *Twilight. Fifty Shades of Gray.* Cultural events so big that people outside the relevant genre had heard of them and rushed in to buy the book. Big movie deals are generally associated with Social reader phenomenon.

You can make a nice living on voracious readers and the casual readers in your genre, if your product and your brand are both professional looking and engaging. (hint hint)

Let's do some math. (Stop whining in the back, you.)

Let's say I sell an ebook novel on Amazon for $5.99. Amazon pays me 68% of cover. (Long story not worth explaining here.) That ebook sale usually nets me $4.07US. A paper book probably nets me about $2.00, if I'm in extended distribution, so I have to sell twice as many, but we'll stay with ebooks, and round down.

$4 per novel.

So let's say I want to make $48,000US per year in writing income. Solidly middle-class in much of this country. That works out nicely to $4,000/month. At $4 per copy, I need to be selling a rough total of one thousand ebook novels each month. My math is weirder, because I have lots of novellas that make me money, plus a bunch of short fiction and the two Book Ones that net me about thirty cents a sale.

If you sell 1,000 novels per month, that works out to about thirty-three novel sales per day. That's it. Thirty-three a day, averaged over a year. Now, selling that many copies of one novel puts you into the top twenty in most Amazon categories. Keep that in mind. But let's say that you have seventeen novels out. And sell two copies of each of those, every day. I do that a lot. And I have a bunch more titles. Suddenly, you're making money and no longer putting on pants.

BUSINESS RULE: *Days I am happy <> Days I am wearing pants.* (Zero overlap Venn Diagram.)

So you don't need much in order to keep your voracious readers happy, because they are always looking for new books. And Casual fans will happily drop a few bucks here and there for your words. It adds up.

But some people decide that the best way to make money is to **Write To Market**. So they put out a *Harry Potter* knockoff. Or realized that for a stretch of time, sparkly teenage vampire stories were selling well, so they wrote one. And it mostly worked. So they wrote more. Eventually, their catalog was sparkly teenage vampire stories.

And then one day, the bottom fell out of the market. No more glittery blood-suckers on the best seller list. Times change.

One part of the reason Writing To Market fails you is that you end up forcing yourself to write something you don't really like, and it comes through in the work. You aren't giggling madly when you wrote it, and the readers can tell. They aren't giggling either. They get bored and put your book down and never come back to finish it or buy the next one.

If you love teenage, sparkly vampire stories more than anything in the universe, you will enjoy writing them, and your prose will be good. People will enjoy you as a writer. But you also have to face the day when the genre falls back to earth. And if your entire career is teenage sparkly vampires, that might be your whole career, especially if you can't bring excited fans with you when you move to writing pulp detective stories.

Because the Writing To Market gig is a track to burnout, because you the writer understands (at least subconsciously) that the market demand is a temporary spike, and not a long-term gig. You end up writing hard and fast and it becomes a job to grind out as many repetitive stories as you can in the shortest period of time.

I've known too many writers who burned themselves out on writing something they didn't enjoy, but they did it because they thought that was where all the money was. Circle back and think about Kindle Unlimited, and that treadmill. Every novel makes you less per share, because more people are sharing the pot every month. And those reader won't come with you somewhere else. When you Write To Market, you run the same risks. Social readers and casual readers, but not fans.

I had to kind of invent the type of Science Fiction I wanted to read, because I could not find it on the shelves at used bookstores. And I looked, trust me. Old Doc Smith stuff. David Drake. C. S. Friedman. Big, action adventury stuff. Most of that product has moved to Indie press and ebooks. I found lots of folks there to read and enjoy, once I knew where to look.

Find the thing that brings you joy to write, and understand the size of your sub-genre. This conversation originally started with my friend lamenting that he couldn't seem to sell a lot of his Steamfunk stories. That's an African-American sub-subgenre of Steam**punk**, which was a big thing ten or fifteen years ago, but has faded back down to where it was thirty years ago. (Sparkly vampires, anyone?) He might have reached all the solid fans (voracious and casual) because that is such a small field of readers.

Okay, done with political opinions. Let's move on to some of the things you can do at a basic, passive-marketing way, to boost your career.

All In

Amazon Ads

Grain of salt warning: *maybe they change the rules soon and this no longer works as well.*

I run ads on Amazon. Not a lot of them and not particularly aggressively, as I want to fire and forget. If you are careful, you won't go broke.

Mine are Sponsored Product ads, rather than what used to be called Product Display and is now apparently Lockscreen. Those latter are the ones that show up on your kindle reader when you power it up and need to get in. Some ad someone has paid for, based on what you have bought in the past or what the buyer wants to target. I have no idea who they think I am, because I get some silly-bad offers.

The ads I do, called Sponsored Product Ads, are easy to do and I recommend you try a few. Name your campaign with the book and the date, so you can find and sort things easy later. (The UI sucks, so you'll end up exporting a file to Excel to read.) Let your campaign run forever for now. (End dates are critical if you are doing a high-spend, spike-driven campaign I have heard called a garden gnome, but this is background noise.) You can always just turn a campaign off later.

Set your daily budget low. I never go above $10, and don't think I have ever actually come close to spending that amount spent.

Keep the default for Automatic targeting for now. (Manual is when you're getting active and trying all sorts of complicated word-game stuff. We want to be still passive. WIBBOW)

Do a custom text ad. You have to boil your blurb down hard (150 characters, I think without looking) and this is where Joseph Sugarman helps you get the right emotional appeal in the fewest words.

Select your title. I suggest either Book One or Book Latest In Series. Either works for different reasons.

Bidding is where it gets interesting. Depending on your genre, the machine will suggest a range for you to pick from. If you have set your daily budget low enough, you can bid a little more aggressively here, because the machine automatically stops when it runs out of money. I suggest you experiment with several titles and see what happens.

You should not go broke on Amazon Ads. Assuming you don't fat-finger anything or get crazy.

Because I'm passive, my ad spend has been small, but my net, reported sales are running more or less 2.5 times my ad spend starting from when I got serious about this six months ago. Set yourself a small budget for this sort of thing and let it play out. Most of you already have such a budget for your print books, and hopefully you've already ordered two sets of business cards, so just add Amazon Ads in and let them percolate in the background. Because Amazon will take the money out before they pay you, you aren't out anything up front.

What I have noticed is that the Amazon algorithm seems to take into account that you are advertising with them. I've seen a broad increase across all titles that I cannot attribute to anything other than the 'bots deciding to be nice to me. (Yeah, sue me.) That and adding more titles in more series on a regular basis, but I'm kinda throwing wet spaghetti at a wall to see what sticks.

It's not much, this growth, but them nickels spend. And it has been solely on Amazon for now, and not showing up particularly on all the other places I sell books.

You will not write the next Hunger Games. (If you do, what lottery numbers do you suggest?) I'm not going to help you become Suzanne Collins, although if you do, I'd appreciate a pull quote I can slap on this cover extolling my genius in helping you. Heh.

What I am trying to do is help you understand the basics of marketing from the perspective of a new publisher just breaking into the business. Running passive Amazon ad campaigns will help.

Signing up for Kobo Promotions will also help. They will not accept you for every, single one, but keep at it and you will get in eventually. The first one won't have any effect, everyone agrees on that topic, but the second or third will seem to break something loose and you'll see a positive return. I doubled my sales (from coffee money to pizza money, granted, but still) this month. And I'll keep at it.

Discoverability

So let's talk about some other things you can do for visibility. Finding readers, or them finding you is the single hardest part of this whole thing, and why you are reading up on marketing. They can be found in many places, but you don't have the time and energy to be everywhere. Bring them to your place for dinner. Being on Amazon and Kobo will help. Being on Social media will help. Looking like a pro will help.

Bundling

There is a new thing in the universe that you need to be familiar with, and many of you aren't.

Bundles are where a reader can buy a whole bunch of stories (usually on a tight theme) for a single, low price. Humble Bundle and Storybundle are two of the big players right now, but they are curated and you kinda hafta know someone to be invited to sit at the big-kids table. I've gotten lucky a few times, but that's just it, luck, more than skill.

BundleRabbit (www.bundlerabbit.com) is a Do-It-Yourself bundling platform. First things first, go put all the stories and novels and collections you have up there. Seriously, right now. I'll wait.

OKAY, so once your stories and novels are in BundleRabbit, someone comes along and decides they want to do a bundle on the theme of Giraffe Detectives, for instance. They have the perfect story. They do looking through the BundleRabbit catalog and find several other stories that would fit.

You get an invite to be in a bundle. You should take it, unless there are good reasons not to.

When the bundle goes live, you advertise it to all your fans, who should have already read your story, but now they can get maybe ten more for a low price, and the theme works. They'll go buy it and discover other writers they might like.

That's the trade. You put up all your fans. I'll put up all mine. We'll both get more fans in the crossover and eventually new sales out of the deal. You won't make money immediately, but you will gain fans, and that means more and better career.

Is your catalog on BundleRabbit yet?

Collaboration

When you get adventurous, BundleRabbit also has an advanced tool called Collaboration. In a straight bundle, everybody splits things evenly, but they also have to have their own covers, blurbs, etc. Proper ebooks.

In a collaboration project, one person organizes things and gets people to put in stories. But those stories don't have to be anything more than Word docs, because the organizer will handle all the formatting and put a cover on this thing that will look like an anthology put out by a professional publisher. And you can even do print books.

Also, you can play with the percentages in how people get paid. This is not a bad thing, as you might be able to invite in a big player and give them a larger share, and the newbies will take a smaller cut, but get the exposure. This is all about exposure.

I edit and publish Boundary Shock Quarterly magazine. (BSQ) (www.boundaryshockquarterly.com). It is a quarterly science fiction anthology/magazine where every issue is on a theme. *Captain's Log. Grand Theft Starship. Tuesday After Next. Ray Guns & Space Babes.* You get the picture.

(I even wrote a Business For Breakfast Books: *How to Launch a Magazine for Professional Publishers* if you want more details on the template I used to do this, the checklists, and the contracts I have with my authors. It's all there for you to replicate, because you can do this thing now.)

In BSQ, BundleRabbit takes a 10% off the top, but everything else is shared. The publisher (Knotted Road Press) gets a 25% cut to cover expenses, art, etc., and the rest of the authors in any given issue split the remaining 75%. If your story is full length (more than 2,000 words, up to 20,000), you get a full share. Flash fiction is a half share.

BundleRabbit handles all the accounting and pays everyone. Did you catch that? I never have to deal with money. I can never be accused of embezzling or co-mingling funds. I get a royalty-share accountant on staff.

Issue 005 of Boundary Shock Quarterly just came out in January 2019, and Issue 006 will be in April. We're doing well enough to justify the effort for me financially, but I'm also sharing fans with a large group of other writers.

You can do the same thing. And it is DIY.

Go get together a group of friends and write some anthologies. And then reach out and invite a couple of near-strangers to participate, so you get to meet new fans who have never heard of you.

Disrupting the Future

MIDDLEMEN SERVICES

Kobo has the easiest upload/publishing user interface I have found. Amazon's is not bad. Some of the other players really need to invest in making their stuff easier to use, because they were poorly thought out a decade ago and haven't been updated.

As a result, middlemen companies have come along to help. As of today (Jan 2019), there are really four significant ebook distributors in the North American market: Amazon, Kobo, Apple/iBooks, and Barnes & Noble. The latter two still don't have their act together, in my opinion, when it comes to wanting to compete with Amazon. Kobo understands and works hard at it. (Whether or not they succeed, they compete, and that makes everyone up their game as a result.)

However, there are a bunch (BUNCH) of other places where you can sell ebooks. And a whole other world where you can sell print books, beyond Amazon. But knowing who those markets are and how to get into them suddenly goes WIBBOW on me, and it should for most of you as well.

Draft To Digital (D2D)

I upload my books directly to Amazon and Kobo. That's it. For EVERYONE else (big and small), I use a company called

Draft To Digital (D2D, https://www.draft2digital.com/). For a small cut (10%, I think but don't quote me), they will handle the effort of getting my ebooks into Apple and B&N, as well as an ever-growing market of international options. Their cut is worth it to me, because that's fewer places I have to deal with, and more options every week I have never heard of before that might generate me fans wanting to buy my book in countries I've never visited, let along imagined might like my brand of SciFi.

Just looking at their website right now, I see these options: Amazon, Apple, B&N, Kobo, Playster, Scribd, Tolino, 24Symbols, OverDrive (Public Libraries), bibliotheca, and Baker & Taylor. That's nine other places where I can sell my books for one upload.

They also have Audio book options, as well as a full suite of editing/publishing tools you can use/hire, including cover designers. (Most writers don't understand what makes good covers. It is something you have to learn and keep up to date. Fabulous Publisher Babe™ is my expert.)

Public Libraries

I mentioned earlier that a lot of people have magic books and library cards now. That means you should get your ebooks into various library systems. There are two ways in, depending on how you do it.

Kobo owns OverDrive these days, so you can get in there from Kobo when you upload your books on that site. D2D is the other place, and part of the reason you should look hard at them. Like I mentioned, I do Amazon and Kobo direct, and usually let D2D handle everything else, and Kobo does my library books as part of that.

Generally, TradPub sells an ebook to a library system for some crazy amount of money (I seem to remember $70 each, or something, for an ebook. Seriously?), because they see libraries as costing them sales elsewhere. The general current recommendation in the indie world as of Jan 2019 is to price your ebooks at three times the retail price for libraries. So if you're selling your book for $4.99, retail, price it at $14.99 for libraries. This lets the library know that you value your work and chances are, it isn't crap. If you then have you fans go into their local libraries and ask for your book, the friendly librarians might look it up and order it because you look as though you know what you're doing (and it isn't absurdly priced like a TradPub novel when they have tight budgets.)

Not all of the readers who discover you in the library will convert to buying your books, because this is largely another source of folks who can't or won't buy books, but they also do tend to buy the occasional book when they find someone they like. That might be you. Or they'll tell a friend about you.

Discoverability is almost equal to throwing wet spaghetti at a wall. Some of it will stick.

GETTING BACK TO D2D, I have an interesting rumor to share. On both B&N and Apple Books (what used to be iBooks), there seems to be a trend evident. Some of the big people who let me sneak into their meetings have reported that they have seen improved sales when putting their books into those two vendors going through D2D. Better sales than when they go directly. Nobody knows why. Given how poor both websites are, I don't have a lot of faith in their back end data warehousing, and that's the sort of thing I did for a living, back in the days when I had a day job.

So that's another reason to consider D2D. Plus Dan and Kevin are smart guys, and really interested in making a lot of money, so they want you to succeed, because they are getting a share, not a fee.

Did you catch that? They are getting a cut of your sales, so it is in their interest to make sure your sales grow. And they're doing the hard work of middlemanning for you, so you have

more time to write. Sure, you could get into all those markets directly and save yourself the money. At the cost of time spent researching new markets and new players ever week, as well as getting everything formatted for them.
WIBBOW.

Would
I
Be
Better
Off
Writing?

I find it worth my time. Your career = your choice. These are new options that get better every day.

Audio

So experts tell me that audio books are the NEXT BIG THING in publishing. And they may even be right. In the past, the only big player was Audible, which is owned by Amazon. And they had ways for Indies like you and me to get into it.

I would do a royalty-share project by auditioning audio talent. (Actually, Fabulous Publisher Babe™ handles all that, so take everything here in the Imperial We, 'cause she's at least half of everything I do, and most of the success.) Once you have a voice talent, I get 20% of sales, they get 20% of sales, and Amazon kept 60%. Which was better than a sharp stick in the eye, but not a lot of money.

These days, there are competitors. Capitalism is forcing the marketplace open and you have options. According to people I know in the audio world, more options will keep appearing over the next year or so, so keep your ears open. (Not a pun. Not really.)

I was at OryCon in Portland, OR last fall, and talked about how I wanted to get aggressive in 2019 about doing a lot of audio, but that I planned on paying the talent up front (work-for-hire, rather than royalty share). I have one series (*The Science Officer*) where the eight books have audio. For the Jessica Keller Chronicles (*Auberon*, et al) I managed to snag a friend who does Books For The Blind as a side gig and she's working her way through them (*Queen Of The Pirates* is out and she's on *Last of the Immortals* now).

But I also have two other series launching this summer, and wanted to be able to drop audio at the same time I drop ebook and print. That's going to happen.

When the panel was done, this dude, who had been sitting back in a corner nodding at me, walked up and handed me his card. He's professional audio talent for hire. (See why you need cards? I can't remember the names of most of the people I met at that con, but I still have his card.)

We actually auditioned a couple of people we met there, because them folks had come to OryCon looking for business and were hungry. That first dude is doing my Star Dragon series, and if it all works out, I'll probably hire him to do my Longshot books as well.

Serendipity, but mixed with professionalism. I knew what I wanted, made it clear, and the right people heard me and stepped up.

So let's talk audio costs.

A novel generally tends to run around 9,000 words per hour spoken, as a broad rule of thumb. It also varies by author, style, and genre, but let's sit there and count. If your novel is 45,000 words, you should expect it to run about five hours to listen to, give or take.

Audio talent gets paid on a rate that is measured in *Finished Hours*. Meaning, the novel is five hours, and they bill you for five hours at the agreed-to rate.

My understanding from pros I have asked is that they spend about 3-4 hours of actual work on every hour of final product, so if you break their billable rate down that way, it doesn't look so bad. And doing it by final product means that they have a vested interest in doing it clean and perfect on the first take, since they can't bill you for the slop.

Once they have the files done, your job is to listen with a copy of your manuscript in hand, following along with your finger. There will be mistakes. Nature of the beast. Good talent catches them before they get to you, but some always sneak through.

(I have even seen situations where I wrote something a little awkwardly and their brain automatically cleaned it up when they read it and we left that as they did it, because it worked better. They also catch mistakes in the source document, like the time I got two characters mixed up and the novel had already gone through four different copy edits and nobody had caught it.)

In the old days, when you were on Audible, you just approved the files and Audible published them. Now, since you have hired your talent, you have the final versions in hand and have sent them money. You can put the files up directly on Audible and get a different payment schedule, or you can put them someplace like Findaway Voices (which is associated with Draft2Digital) and let them handle the delivery for you.

Oh, and did I mention that Findaway Voices is similar to D2D, in that they're a distributor? By going through them, you're actually putting your audiobook up on a dozen other platforms, such as iTunes, Audible, as well as B&N and Scribd.

That's why we talked about D2D and the middleman concept first. There are other middlemen out there who are coming up fast, like Streetlib or PublishDrive but I haven't used them, mostly due to Fabulous Publisher Babe's™ own WIBBOW, so I don't know if they are better or worse. I do know Dan and Kevin and Ricardo personally, and many folks who have worked with them, and they all have good things to say.

The reason audio is growing is because people are already into podcasts, and used to listening to their entertainment. My brain doesn't work that way, but a lot of people love it. Hell, some people are just having their home surveillance units (Alexa, Google, etc.) read them the book from the ebook file, because they can't get enough audio books to listen to.

This is a market you can tap. Depending on how you go into it, it might not cost you much up front, either. You decide. I am transitioning to work for hire, but I also was able to negotiate a good deal with this new guy, because I promised him five novels up front, all done right now so he could just go through all of them at once. With the chance of a whole other series after that.

What you will pay your audio talent is fluid, and subject to your ability to negotiate, balanced against them maybe being fans of your work. They get paid on the finished hour. Depending, you should expect to pay around $250 per finished hour for quality work. For amazing people, that can go up. For new folks just breaking in, it will probably be lower. If you offer them consistent work (like I have eleven novels in two series right now that I want audio, and the cash in hand to pay you half now and half on completion), you can probably get a pretty good deal.

Make sure you audition them. You send a section from the beginning, like chapter one, and they'll record you a quick sample (maybe 1-2 pages give or take) for you to listen to. We auditioned several people for the Star Dragon. One came across as almost bored reading the work. That was bad, because that will cause the listener to get bored.

We hired the guy we did because he read the books and was jazzed enough to want to know how the whole thing (5 novels) went. His voice sounded excited to read, and that sort of thing infectiously draws the listener in as well. *OMG What happens NEXT?*

Also, when you do the final contract, they won't be long. I think ours was 2 pages. Just a clear note that this is work-for-hire and the audio talent has no rights to the final product after they get paid, though they own the copyright. (Remember, copyright is based on FORM. If you don't understand that, you need to go educate yourself on copyright IMMEDIATELY. This is your business. Licensing copyright makes you money. You must know what makes you money in your business.) Pay Rate. Deadlines. If they get long and complicated, take a long, hard look at it before you sign, and make sure there's nothing in there you find objectionable.

BUSINESS RULE I LEARNED FROM MY FATHER: *Contracts are not for when things go right. They are for when things go wrong. ALWAYS have a contract signed if money is changing hands. I don't care if they are your best friend since kindergarten.*

So I plan to expand my offerings to folks via audio this year. Hopefully, the break-even point is in the short term, and not measured in years and years.

Translations

The other place I am working to expand my reach in 2019 is translation. My Science Officer series are a set of novellas, 24-32,000 words each. Quick read. Long story arc. Interesting space pirates.

Given that as a starting point, I wanted to get them into German. The German fan base for science fiction is huge, and they like long arcs of stories that they can read quickly. The Perry Rhodan books are all generally novellas in length. The publisher has put out a new one every week **since 1961**. We're approaching sixty years of weekly science fiction story. There have been retcons, reboots, and spin-offs, but they hit the BILLION books sold mark in about 1984, I think, and are close or maybe past TWO BILLION.

We're betting that means that I have a built-in fan base that I hope to reach.

Depending on the genre (there it is again) that your writer works in, you ought to be able to see success in other languages, but I can't tell you what they are. Some genre translate well, others don't. Some cultures read and others don't.

Do your homework and understand what novel you think will translate well and sell ahead of time.

As of right now, I am using Language+ Literary Translations (http://www.literarytranslations.us) and they have been good to work with. In fact, after we had a contract in place for *The Science Officer*, Kobo announced that they were partnering with Language+ to offer translation as a service, so I feel even better. (Someone I regard highly originally recommended these folks, and I owe the man a beer next time I see him.)

Epilogue: 2019

What works?

It's the beginning of 2019. The purpose of this book was to give you a checklist, as a small-press, Indie publisher looking at the huge list of things you might do. Like I said before, doing these things won't guarantee you success, but not understanding them probably ends in failure. You want to come across as a professional when you randomly run into someone that might be able to help your career, like the audio-dude who could walk up and hand me his card when I was looking and he happened to have walked into that panel.

Serendipity.

Or you're sitting in a restaurant, talking publishing, like Fabulous Publisher Babe™ and I do constantly, and the waitress says "Oh, you're a writer? What do you write?" and the marketing card comes out. (She still has it, too.)

I expect narrowcasting to overtake the big social media players soon. They won't collapse, but they won't have the reach and social heft they once did, so you won't be able to reach as many people as you used to. It's still a good way to remain in touch, and to channel people back to your actual website, so that if they do go away, you aren't f@#$%d.

Epilogue: 2019

As a new publisher, or an old publisher discovering that the world has changed, you need to be aware of what it takes to look like a pro, and how to punch above your weight. (I do that all the time, especially when talking to folks who might make six figures in sales **monthly**. But I look to the future and we all have things to learn from one another.)

Some of the things I have listed here won't work for you. That's fine. You are responsible for your own career. If you look at one of my suggestions and decide I'm completely full of shit, do it your way. (And send me a note detailing why and what you did to make it work so I can update future editions or other books for people with a career arc more like yours than mine, please?)

Everyone has a different path to the top of the mountain. Not only that, there are a hell of a lot of mountain tops out there to reach. A lot of my success has come from me writing in the particular genre I do (science fiction) and the way I grew up reading comic books when I was a kid, so I already see story in long arcs. And the fact that I had to study and understand genre as a tool before I wrote something, so I don't tend to slipstream into strange places that are hard to describe to a potential reader.

There are tools and services out there that can help you with the middleman tasks that fall between you finishing your manuscript and it being bought by someone in Tanzania. Figure out how much of that work you want to do yourself, and what you should farm out to third parties. There exists an entire ecosystem now, people who make a living doing editing, formatting, covers, and audio, plus lots of other things. I have a grand-niece I want to hire, one of these days, because she's going to grow up as a marketing and business shark, and she's got the mindset to make a killing at something like that when she's old enough that her mother will let me corrupt her with money.

However, and this is the BUT! part, **when you hire someone**, look at other customers they have. Ask for references.

A pro will have them available. A conman will get offended at the question. Get multiple bids, unless this is someone that you trust or can rely on someone else's prior validation. Audition audio talent and listen with your eyes closed, rather than looking at what they might cost you.

It is your career on the line here. All these others will be hired for short-term gigs or shares of your eventual sales, but it is your name on the cover of that book, and you need to make all those decisions with that in mind. I want thirty more years of writing (I'm already kinda an old fart these days), so I look with that sort of vision.

BUSINESS RULE: Unrelated, but important, since we were talking about your long-term career, always make sure you control the money. Sign your own checks, rather than relying on the kindness of someone else to handle your money. This is doubly important when you get to be big enough that those monthly royalty checks have commas in them.

Someone asked what that meant. "Sign your own checks." It means do not trust that someone else has your best interests at heart for money. Have it all come to you, your bank accounts, and then you send it out as necessary. I've heard too many horror stories of agents robbing even big name authors (BNA) blind by having the money come to the agent, rather than the writer, and then just sending on things when they wanted. Everyone works for you, not the other way around. You get the money. You control the money. You pay them for services after they have completed contract terms, and not before.

You are responsible for your own career. We can help, but we can't want your success more than you do. I can offer advice and tips. You need to read them, analyze them, and make your own decisions.

My suggestion, however, is to give more credence to the people who are successful, measured in cashflow. They are doing something right. The dilettante at the café might have all sorts of nifty ideas about what I'm doing wrong, but until he's making good money in Indie, I will take all his advice with a pinch of salt. (I'll listen, because every person I have ever met in my life had something useful to teach me, even if it was what NOT to do.)

Why this book?

My corporate mission statement, paraphrased: *Build a longer table instead of a higher fence.* Help others who are not as far along in their careers. Show them doors that they didn't even know existed, so that they can walk up and kick the fucker in. I've gotten the pleasure of watching that happen a couple of times, and there is no greater feeling in the world than watching someone suddenly figure out how to be happy and successful at their art when they had been trapped in a box too small.

You are responsible for your own career. I will keep repeating that. My rules are not rules. They are checklists for you to read and discard as necessary. But you need to have a reason before ignoring those ideas. They have worked for me, so there is something there, and I hope it at least gives you better ideas.

We have talked about very basic things here, but nobody seems to be teaching some of these things to new writers just breaking into the field and trying to become publishers. I'll do an Intermediate book later, where I'll go into some of the next level things you can try, but there's enough here for many people working on their first half-dozen novels to digest.

If you have other suggestions or ideas, please send them my way. I'll either update this book or write another one as the world changes.

You are not my competition. Seriously.

This is not pie. My being successful (getting a larger slice, as it were) does not cost you anything. In fact, if I grow the pie by getting more people to read, and helping more writers to look good, then we'll all come out ahead.

My purpose is to help other artists. That's not necessarily your gig, and that's fine as well.

Epilogue: 2019

We'll all get to the top of the mountain by our own road. Now, go write your next book.

shade and sweet water,
    blaze
    20190129
    West of the Mountains, WA

Read More!

Be sure to pick up the other books in the Business for Breakfast series!

The Beginning Professional Writer
The Beginning Professional Publisher
The Beginning Professional Storyteller
The Intermediate Professional Storyteller
Business Planning for Professional Publishers
The Healthier Professional Writer
The Three Act Structure for Professional Writers
How to Launch a Magazine for Professional Publishers
Pulp Speed for the Professional Writer
Growing as a Professional Artist
Beginning Marketing For The Professional Publisher
Covers for the Professional Publisher

About the Author

Blaze Ward writes science fiction in the Alexandria Station universe (Jessica Keller, The Science Officer, The Story Road, etc.) as well as several other science fiction universes, such as Star Dragon, the Collective, and more. He also writes odd bits of high fantasy with swords and orcs. In addition, he is the Editor and Publisher of *Boundary Shock Quarterly Magazine*. You can find out more at his website www.blazeward.com, as well as Facebook, Goodreads, and other places.

Blaze's works are available as ebooks, paper, and audio, and can be found at a variety of online vendors (Kobo, Amazon, and others). His newsletter comes out quarterly, and you can also follow his blog on his website. He really enjoys interacting with fans, and looks forward to any and all questions—even ones about his books!

Never miss a release!
If you'd like to be notified of new releases, sign up for my newsletter.

I will never spam you or use your email for nefarious purposes. You can also unsubscribe at any time.

http://www.blazeward.com/newsletter/

Connect with Blaze!

Web: www.blazeward.com
Boundary Shock Quarterly (BSQ):
https://www.boundaryshockquarterly.com/

- facebook.com/KRPBlaze
- goodreads.com/Blaze_Ward

About Knotted Road Press

Knotted Road Press fiction specializes in dynamic writing set in mysterious, exotic locations.

Knotted Road Press non-fiction publishes autobiographies, business books, cookbooks, and how-to books with unique voices.

Knotted Road Press creates DRM-free ebooks as well as high-quality print books for readers around the world.

With authors in a variety of genres including literary, poetry, mystery, fantasy, and science fiction, Knotted Road Press has something for everyone.

Knotted Road Press
www.KnottedRoadPress.com

www.ingramcontent.com/pod-product-compliance
Lightning Source LLC
Chambersburg PA
CBHW071114030426
42336CB00013BA/2071